POUND'S ARTISTS

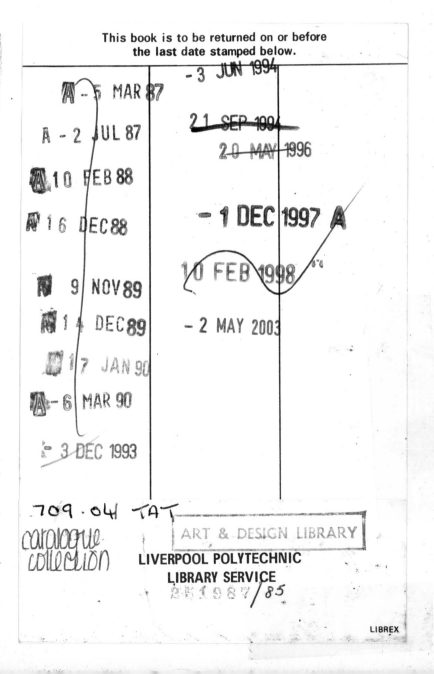

POUND'S ARTISTS

Ezra Pound and the Visual Arts in
London, Paris and Italy

THE TATE GALLERY

front cover/jacket
Wyndham Lewis, **Ezra Pound**, 1939 (detail)
Tate Gallery

frontispiece
Ezra Pound, 1918, photograph: E. O. Hoppé
Mansell Collection

Published to coincide with an exhibition held at
Kettle's Yard Gallery, University of Cambridge, 14 June – 4 August 1985,
and the Tate Gallery 11 September – 10 November 1985. Organised by Kettle's Yard,
the Cambridge Poetry Festival Society and the Tate Gallery with financial
assistance for the Kettle's Yard showing from the Arts Council of Great Britain,
the Cambridge Festival Association and Faber and Faber.

Photographic Credits
David Clarke; The Conway Library, London; Michael Duffet;
The Fitzwilliam Museum, Cambridge; Kettle's Yard Gallery, Cambridge;
David Lambert; The Mansell Collection; Robert G. Mates; David Runnacles;
Tate Gallery Publications and Scala/Firenze.

ISBN 0 946590 26 5 (paper)
ISBN 0 946590 28 1 (cloth)
Copyright © 1985 The Tate Gallery All rights reserved
Designed and published by Tate Gallery Publications,
Millbank, London SW1P 4RG
Printed in Great Britain by Balding + Mansell Limited,
Wisbech, Cambs

Contents

Foreword

The exhibition *Pound's Artists*, and this publication which accompanies it, celebrate the centenary of the birth of the poet Ezra Pound. Both the Cambridge Poetry Festival and the Tate Gallery had considered a Pound exhibition for 1985, and we have been happy to collaborate under the aegis of Kettle's Yard, University of Cambridge, which has arranged the exhibition, and has our grateful thanks.

We remember Pound as the life-long lover of art, and especially as the friend of Wyndham Lewis and Gaudier-Brzeska, whose portraits of the poet dominate the exhibition. It should never be forgotten that Pound invented the word Vorticism, and was one of the most stalwart supporters of modern art in Britain. And at the Tate Gallery – 'that sink of abomination' as Pound later called it when he was campaigning for the 'new' – we like to think of the young Pound excited by our Whistler exhibition of 1912, which started him thinking about art and the position of the artist, especially if he were an American-born expatriate determined to settle in Europe.

Pound remained deeply interested in the visual arts, as his large output of criticism and many references in the poetry make clear. The essays in this book approach Pound's interest by looking at his involvement with the visual arts in the three places – London, Paris and Italy – in which he successively lived. Although it is not, strictly speaking, a catalogue, the book deals mainly with the paintings, sculpture, photography and printed material in the exhibition to which it relates.

Thanks are due, first of all, to the authors of the essays that follow who are also the selectors of the exhibition: John Alexander, Richard Humphreys and Peter Robinson; and to Clive Wilmer of the Cambridge Poetry Festival Society, who has made important contributions to the shape of both the exhibition and this book. Hilary Gresty and her staff at Kettle's Yard have worked tirelessly to realise the project. Most of the work in the exhibition comes from the collections of Kettle's Yard and the Tate Gallery which have important holdings of the artists with whom Pound was most closely associated, particularly of Gaudier-Brzeska and of Wyndham Lewis.

We are also very grateful for the generosity of Anthony d'Offay and those members of the Pound family, notably Omar Pound, Olga Rudge and Mary de Rachewiltz, whose important loans and interest and support have made such an outstanding contribution to the exhibition.

Alan Bowness *Director, Tate Gallery.*

Acknowledgements

Many people have contributed to the organisation of the exhibition *Pound's Artists* and to the preparation of this accompanying publication. We would like to extend our special thanks to: Walter Bauman, John Bodley, Pavel Büchler, Louisa Buck, Barrie Bullen, Richard Cork, Andrew Cross, Sue Duncan, Serge Fauchereau, Christopher Green, Patricia Hutchins, Annely Juda, Lionel Kelly, Harold Landry, Jeremy Lewison, Madeleine Marsh, Andrew Nairne, Sara Pappworth, Graham Pollard, and Simon Wilson.

In particular we would like to thank Helen Dore for her tireless work as both copy-editor and proof-reader of this book; and also Penny Wheeler, who put immense effort into locating artworks, books and magazines.

The exhibition has been generously supported by the Cambridge Festival Association, Eastern Arts Association and Faber and Faber. Kettle's Yard is, as always, grateful for the generous support of the Arts Council of Great Britain.

Lenders to the Exhibition

Heiner Bastian
Birmingham Museum and City Art Gallery
Ivor Braka Ltd
The British Library
The Syndics of Cambridge University Library
Anthony D'Offay Gallery Ltd
The Syndics of the Fitzwilliam Museum
Ex Libris
Mark Glazebrook
The Trustees of the Cecil Higgins Art Gallery
Lionel Kelly
Quentin Keynes
University of London Library
Manchester City Art Galleries
National Museum of Wales
University of Reading, Department of English
University of Reading Library
The Royal Photographic Society
Victoria and Albert Museum, Department of Prints and Drawings
Private Collections

Bibliographical Note

Most of Ezra Pound's writings on the visual arts are collected in *Ezra Pound and the Visual Arts* (New York, 1980), edited with an introduction by Harriet Zinnes. In the notes to the essays in this book all references to Pound's works are taken, where possible, from recent editions. A full reference is given for the first mention of a book in each essay and subsequent references are to an abbreviated title, in the case of Pound's work, or to the author's surname. Unless otherwise stated all articles referred to are by Pound.

Most of Ezra Pound's poetry and translations can be found in the following publications:

> *Collected Early Poems*, New York, 1976
> *Collected Shorter Poems*, London, 1984
> *The Cantos*, London, 1975
> *The Translations of Ezra Pound*, London, 1984
> *The Classic Anthology defined by Confucius*, London, 1974

The most important prose works by Pound are:

> *The Spirit of Romance*, London, 1910
> *Gaudier-Brzeska: A Memoir*, London, 1916
> *Pavannes and Divisions*, New York, 1918
> *Instigations*, New York, 1920
> *Antheil and the Treatise on Harmony*, Paris, 1924
> *ABC of Economics*, London, 1933
> *ABC of Reading*, London, 1934
> *Make it New*, London, 1934
> *Jefferson and/or Mussolini*, London, 1935
> *Guide to Kulchur*, London, 1938
> *Literary Essays of Ezra Pound*, London, 1954
> *Confucius: The Great Digest, The Unwobbling Pivot, The Analects*, New York, 1969
> *Selected Prose*, London, 1973

A full bibliography of Pound can be found in: Donald Gallup, *A Bibliography of Ezra Pound*, New York, 1983. A useful brief bibliography can be found in: Peter Ackroyd, *Ezra Pound and his World*, London, 1980.

Introduction

RICHARD HUMPHREYS

'To build the city of Dioce whose terraces are the colour of stars.'[1]

Ezra Pound was born in Hailey, Idaho, USA, in 1885. After studying at the University of Pennsylvania and at Hamilton College in Utica he travelled in Europe in 1906 to study the writings of Lope de Vega and the Provençal poets. In 1908 he went to Venice and then moved to London where he was based until 1920. There he built a career as a poet and literary scholar; he was taken up by W. B. Yeats and quickly became a central figure in contemporary English literature. During these important years he was involved not only with the world of letters but also with those visual artists of London he called 'moderns', namely, Wyndham Lewis, Edward Wadsworth, Henri Gaudier-Brzeska and Frederick Etchells, who, in Pound's opinion, were the most important artists in the movement he called 'Vorticism'. Pound also championed artists who, by choice or otherwise, were not directly involved in Vorticism, such as the sculptor Jacob Epstein, the photographer Alvin Langdon Coburn, and Dorothy Shakespear whom he married in April 1914.[2] These years were the most significant for Pound as art critic and theorist. He wrote specifically about the artists who interested him, watched them at work, discussed ideas with them and helped to promote their careers. Apart from being an important contributor to the Vorticist periodical *Blast*, Pound also found a patron for 'his' artists in John Quinn, the American lawyer who made possible an exhibition of their work in New York in 1917.

Pound moved to Paris in 1920. London, by then, seemed to him culturally moribund, and he looked to the French capital for a new milieu in which to exercise his talents as writer and impresario. His interests here were still in the 'moderns' and included the work of Francis Picabia, Constantin Brancusi and Fernand Léger. He was briefly involved in the Dada movement and also became interested in avant-garde cinema. It was at this time that he began to research the life of the Italian renaissance despot, Sigismundo Malatesta, for the early parts of his ambitious long historical poem, *The Cantos*, begun during the war. For Pound Paris offered a continuation of the enthusiasms he had developed in London, but it never really provided him with such a coherent arena of activity nor with such a sympathetically inclined group of artists.

In 1924 he moved to Rapallo in Italy with his wife Dorothy, and was followed by

THE LEWIS-BRZESKA-POUND TROUPE.
Blasting their own trumpets before the walls of Jericho.

Horace Brodsky, 'The Lewis – Brzeska – Pound Troupe' (lost),
reproduced in *The Egoist* (15 July 1914)

the violinist Olga Rudge, who was to become the other woman in Pound's life. Henceforth, until 1945, Pound worked on *The Cantos*, which were published in instalments, and also wrote prose works such as *Guide to Kulchur*, *ABC of Reading*, *ABC of Economics* and *Social Credit: an Impact*. From the end of the Great War Pound became obsessed by politics and economics and was an exponent of the economic theories of Major C. H. Douglas. Douglas had invented a new monetary order based on a federal loan system which he called Social Credit, which sought to eradicate usury or the excessive profit made by individual lenders.[3] Pound used Douglas's ideas to criticise contemporary Western culture, to place the artist in a social and economic context, and to develop a means by which to judge the comparative 'health' of any epoch's art. For example, he saw the art of the Quattrocento in Italy, which he characterised as linear and 'clean', as the product of a relatively non-usurious period; whereas the Seicento, with its baroque *sfumato* and 'fleshiness', was the typical expression of a corrupt and commercialised culture. Quite early in *The Cantos* the imagery addresses itself savagely to the 'unnatural' results of financial power vested in individual hands.

> The slough of unamiable liars,
> > bog of stupidities,
> malevolent stupidities, and stupidities,
> the soil living pus, full of vermin,
> dead maggots begetting live maggots,
> > slum owners,
> usurers squeezing crab-lice, pandars to authority,

rising to an obscene crescendo, with Grosz-like venom,

> And Invidia,
> the corruptio, foetor, fungus
> liquid animals, melted ossifications,
> slow rot, foetid combustion,
> > chewed cigar-butts, without dignity, without tragedy,
> . . . in Episcopus, waving a condom full of black-beetles,
> monopolists, obstructors of knowledge,
> > obstructors of distribution.[4]

In many respects Pound, like his mentor Douglas, owed more than he acknowledged to the arguments of the nineteenth-century art and social theorist, John Ruskin. These ideas were paralleled during this part of Pound's career by his commitment to Fascist politics and in particular to Benito Mussolini whose Fascist state, Pound believed, could inaugurate his own preferred economic reforms and would create a productive atmosphere for artists. In both cases he was disappointed.

During World War II Pound broadcast, for Rome Radio, his own political propaganda to America and, in an ornate, sometimes malicious and incomprehensible language, attacked, among other things, the Jews, American politicians and the capitalist economies of the Allies. In April 1945 he was arrested by American troops and, in May, incarcerated in a detention camp in Pisa on a charge of treason. It was here, locked in a cage, that he wrote what many consider to be his finest poetry, *The Pisan Cantos*. He was flown to Washington in November to be charged but was declared unfit for trial on the grounds of insanity. He was committed to St Elizabeth's mental hospital where he remained until 1958 when his indictment for treason was dismissed after a concerted effort by friends to clear his name. While at St Elizabeth's Pound continued to write sections of *The Cantos*, to hold court to a growing number of acolytes and to correspond with friends and admirers across the world. The controversial award in 1949 of the Bollingen Prize for his *Pisan Cantos* divided the intellectual world.[5]

From 1958 until his death in Venice in 1972 Pound lived in Italy, making occasional trips to London, Paris and New York. He continued to write, but these final years of his life were notable for his comparative silence and reclusiveness. His reputation as a poet, scholar and political figure has since been hotly disputed. For some he is one of the most significant modernist writers of the twentieth century, while for others he is an obscurantist charlatan as well as a ferociously anti-semitic apologist for evil and dangerous political theories.[6]

Ezra Pound's *wanderlust* led him not only to settle in Europe but also to explore its past as well as that of China and America. Although his sometime friend and colleague Wyndham Lewis doubted the poet's grasp of the 'here and now', Pound saw his time-travel as a search for a tradition which could, and should, enrich the present. There was never, from his point of view, a problem in admiring Picabia and the Dadaist 'young of Zurich' as well as Agostino di Duccio and Chinese painting of the Sung period. For instance, he writes in 1930, 'There is a Cosimo Tura in Bergamo which Arp has probably never seen. Arp's admirers will probably admire it more than any spectators have during the intermediate period.'[7] He looked for certain common denominators which gave such eclectic tastes cohesion and which, in fact, gave them greater resonance and significance than more circumscribed tastes could ever allow. In Pound's universe the living powers of the past return with faltering steps, they intersect and cast light and shade on the chimeras of the present.

> In the crisp air,
> the discontinuous gods;[8]

For Pound the paradox of this 'return' – as if the past could 'come back' to the present – was a vital source of his vision. A pagan tradition, 'without hell-obsession', trips its way, with threatening sensuality, across the obstacles of a ruined Christian culture,

> . . . the deathless,
> Form, forms and renewal, gods held in the air,
> Forms seen, and then clearness.
> Bright void, without image, Napishtim,
> Casting his gods back into the *νόος*[9]

VORTEX.

POUND.

The vortex is the point of maximum energy,

It represents, in mechanics, the greatest efficiency.

We use the words " greatest efficiency " in the precise sense—as they would be used in a text book of MECHANICS.

You may think of man as that toward which perception moves. You may think of him as the TOY of circumstance, as the plastic substance RECEIVING impressions.

OR you may think of him as DIRECTING a certain fluid force against circumstance, as CONCEIVING instead of merely observing and reflecting.

THE PRIMARY PIGMENT.

The vorticist relies on this alone ; on the primary pigment of his art, nothing else.

Every conception, every emotion presents itself to the vivid consciousness in some primary form.

It is the picture that means a hundred poems, the music that means a hundred pictures, the most highly energized statement, the statement that has not yet SPENT itself it expression, but which is the most capable of expressing.

THE TURBINE.

All experience rushes into this vortex. All the energized past, all the past that is living and worthy to live. All MOMENTUM, which is the past bearing upon us, RACE, RACE-MEMORY, instinct charging the PLACID, NON-ENERGIZED FUTURE.

The DESIGN of the future in the grip of the human vortex. All the past that is vital, all the past that is capable of living into the future, is pregnant in the vortex, NOW.

Hedonism is the vacant place of a vortex, without force, deprived of past and of future, the vertex of a stil spool or cone.

Futurism is the disgorging spray of a vortex with no drive behind it, DISPERSAL.

'Vortex. Pound' from *Blast 1*, July 1914

Painting and sculpture made visible this constant renewal of 'the deathless, form'. 'I have been credited with reviving a *lost* world of sensibility', he wrote.[10] Pound applauded the Victoria and Albert Museum's catholic acquisition policy, but he loathed its tomblike fustiness and architectural triviality. A 'living' museum in a fine building – this is a spatial image of what he intended *The Cantos* to be. By the early twenties Pound had located the source of the problem in economic factors. London, the Victoria and Albert, the Royal Academy, the sculptures on the Ritz were symbols of a 'private culture' (of albums, portfolios, cabinets), suffocating in the mendacious excrescences of a public world mostly 'formed' by usurious finance. The 'great' artists of the age, the Gaudiers, Brancusis and Lewises, are starved or ignored, not out of malice but out of fear – the fear that they might erode this political and aesthetic prison from within.

> The British are the most timorous people on earth in any matter of aesthetics. And the nation will get no buildings worth seeing, it will have no 'new age of cathedrals', until it takes a chance on the 'maniacs'.[11]

This isolation was by no means a bad thing if the arts were in some way effective. 'Nobody has heard of the abstract mathematicians who worked out the determinants that Marconi made use of in his computations for the wireless telegraph,'[12] Pound wrote in 1913, by analogy establishing his 'serious artist' as a potent force in society at large.

For many avant-garde artists the relation of art to life in early twentieth-century Europe highlighted a cultural sickness. Pound, like his artist colleagues, saw the oriental attitude to art as a much-needed model for the West. Laurence Binyon, an early mentor of Pound upon the latter's arrival in London, had written, 'if our art ails, it is because our life ails',[13] and Ernest Fenollosa, perhaps one of the most important influences on Pound during his entire life, had envisaged a 'universal scheme or logic of art' which would bring 'harmony' to life.[14] This is, perhaps, Ruskin 'orientalised'. But Pound insisted that a transformed social and economic order was necessary if such a vision were not to lapse into impractical beauty-worship.

Pound's proposal for a College of Arts in a major American city, such as New York or Chicago, was his first serious attempt to rejuvenate the arts, by the 'mingling of young men in all the different sorts of art', and to get it back into 'life'. Although nothing came of the idea, the College of Arts, like the shortlived Rebel Art Centre, shows how ambitious Pound was for art and artists.[15]

Pound's writings on painting, sculpture and architecture are not those of a professional art historian or aesthetician. He had preferences which expressed themselves in a sometimes bewildering eclectic taste. The preferences, however, seem to have a shape and consistency. He liked linearity and a sense of 'clarity' and

[18]

cleanness in a painting, sculpture or building. 'Carving' might be the best word to describe this preference and could encompass a painting by Uccello or Wyndham Lewis, a sculpture by Agostino or Brancusi, a building by Alberti or Sant'Elia. There is a respect for the particular material the artist uses that Pound favours, and he has a love of the Mediterranean light that enhances the impact of the material and its handling. These preferences have important connections with other concepts and highlights in the Poundian scheme of things. Direct carving into a resistant material is analogous to the eye and mind directing their energies into the chaos of the material world in clear lines and formal intersections; to the poet's cutting into time with image and rhythm; it is like the ploughman digging his furrow; it is the imposition of the will of an individual over an epoch, a country or a people; it is like the assertive male possessing a passive female. As in the case of Wyndham Lewis, Pound adopted the 'male' creative principle, believing as he did in the fundamental power of the *logos spermatikos*, or seminal thought.

Two often converging themes form consistent strands throughout Pound's writings on the visual arts. One is his debt to nineteenth-century art and literature, the other is his love of Italy, and Venice in particular. Pound's imagination was steeped in the work of writers such as Browning, Ruskin, Pater and Rossetti. An obsession with Italy and an intense concern for the moment of aesthetic perception and gratification are connecting features of all their writings. In the case of Ruskin we may even have a direct precedent for Pound's ideas about usury, the decline of taste and his concern with the revival of craft values. In the case of Pater, as with Pound's first artistic hero, Whistler, the transcendent vision of the artist separates him from most men and makes him able, in favourable circumstances, to transform the visible world. Even though Pound became a 'modernist' he never lost a nostalgic affection for the Pre-Raphaelites and for Whistler and the 'Aesthetic' artists who were all forerunners of the modernism Pound espoused. Pound's past did not begin in the Quattrocento but in the late nineteenth century.

Pound's first collection of verse, *A Lume Spento*, was published in Venice in 1908. He never forgot the beauty of Venice, its light, watery setting, buildings and art. Canto III begins,

> I sat on the Dogana's steps
> For the gondolas cost too much, that year.[16]

Pound's lost paradise was Italy and his eventual move there in 1925 signified a return to his spiritual homeland. The social, economic and artistic lives of the Renaissance city-states became criteria by which Pound saw his own times. Malatesta, Medici and Gonzaga were the powerful rulers and patrons whom Pound resurrected as models for the present; and the artists they encouraged, such

Matteo de' Pasti, 'Castle at Rimini', 1446
Syndics of the Fitzwilliam Museum

as Piero della Francesca, Agostino and Mantegna, were not just dead masters to be copied but rather 'living forces' to be revered, studied and emulated. Like Ruskin, Pound believed that a point had come in European history, around 1500, when social conditions changed, and that this change had been determined mostly by the rise of banking. Art subsequently declined in quality and power and became a luxury rather than a part of life. This myth of a fall from some previous state of grace underlies much of the elaborate historical jigsaw puzzle worked on in *The Cantos* and his prose works.

The three essays in this catalogue attempt to chart, in chronological and geographical sequence, Pound's interest in the visual arts – from the frenetic days in London and Paris to a more sedate voluntary exile in Italy. The modern artists dealt with are those with whom Pound had close connections or affinities and about whom he wrote extensively.[17] The final essay deals, primarily, with Renaissance Italian art, mostly as it appears in Pound's poetry and critical essays. After 1925 Pound was no longer part of a group and did not promote a true avant-garde. He wrote, in 1956, 'During the past half-century I have fought for 3 artists . . . Gaudier-Brzeska, Wyndham Lewis, Brancusi.'[18] As *The Pisan Cantos* show,

Dorothy Shakespear, cover for *Ripostes*, 1915

Wyndham Lewis, design for 'Timon of Athens', 1912

mixing history with personal reminiscence, Pound's happiest years were spent in London between 1909 and 1914.

> And also near the museum they served it mit Schlag
> in those days (pre 1914)
> the loss of that café
> meant the end of a B.M. era
> (British Museum era)
> Mr Lewis had been to Spain
> Mr Binyon's young prodigies
> pronounced the word: Penthesilea
> There were mysterious figures
> that emerged from recondite recesses
> and ate at the WIENER CAFÉ
> which died into banking . . .[19]

This had been an age when scholarship (the British Museum), learned elders (Mr Binyon), adventurous youth (Mr Lewis and the young prodigies) and pleasure (the Vienna Café in New Oxford Street) had come together to promise great things. Pound, like Wyndham Lewis, believed the Great War had destroyed a coming

'New Age'. *The Cantos* nostalgically venerate this period, along with the Renaissance and ancient China which had also witnessed 'privileged' moments when the body politic, disregarding its tendencies towards corruption and violence, had allowed itself the indulgence of 'beauty'.

> Great art does not depend upon comfort, it does not depend upon the support of riches. But a great age is brought about only with the aid of wealth, because a great age means the deliberate fostering of genius, the gathering in and grouping and encouragement of artists.[20]

Notes

1 Canto LXXIV, *The Cantos of Ezra Pound*, 3rd edn (London, 1975), p.425.
2 Cantos VIII–XI, *ibid.*, pp.28–41.
3 For Douglas's theories see J. L. Finlay, *Social Credit: The English Origins* (Montreal, 1972).
4 Canto XIV, *ibid.*, p.63.
5 See Harry M. Meacham, *The Caged Panther: Ezra Pound at St Elizabeth's* (New York, 1967).
6 For a recent discussion of Pound's political ideas see Peter Nicholls, *Ezra Pound. Politics, Economics and Writing* (London, 1984).
7 'Epstein, Belgion and Meaning', *The Criterion* (April 1930), pp.470–5 (*Ezra Pound and the Visual Arts*, ed. Harriet Zinnes (New York, 1980), p.164).
8 Canto XXI, *Cantos*, p.99.
9 Canto XXV, *ibid.*, p.119.
10 'Total War on "Contemplatio"', *Edge* (October 1956), pp.19–20 (Zinnes, p.178).
11 'The Curse', *Apple (of Beauty and Discord)* (January 1920), pp.22, 24 (Zinnes, p.160).
12 'The Serious Artist', *Literary Essays of Ezra Pound*, ed. T. S. Eliot (London, 1954), p.47.
13 Laurence Binyon, *Painting in the Far East*, 2nd edn (London, 1913), p.272.
14 See Hugh Kenner, *The Pound Era* (London, 1975), p.239.

15 'America: Chances and Remedies. Proposition III–The College of Arts', *The New Age* (29 May 1913), pp.115–16 (Zinnes, p.3). See also Zinnes, p.275 and Noel Stock, *The Life of Ezra Pound* (Harmondsworth, 1985), pp.212–13.
16 Canto III, *Cantos*, p.11.
17 For this reason a number of artists Pound admired, notably David Bomberg, William Roberts and Laurence Atkinson, will not be discussed in this book of essays. Pound's wife, Dorothy Shakespear, illustrated the covers of two editions of his poems (*Catholic Anthology*, 1915 and *Ripostes*, 1915) and made Vorticist paintings (see Richard Cork, *Vorticism and Abstract Art in the First Machine Age*, 2 vols. (London, 1976), vol.1, pp.286–9), but was never discussed by her husband in his criticism. For their early relationship and interests in art see *Ezra Pound and Dorothy Shakespear: Their Letters, 1909–1914*, ed. Omar Pound and A. Walton Litz (London, 1985).
18 'Total War on "Contemplatio"', pp.19–20 (Zinnes, p.177).
19 Canto LXXX, *Cantos*, p.506.
20 'The Renaissance', *Literary Essays*, p.221.

Colour Plates

Jacob Epstein, 'Female Figure in Flenite', 1913, *Tate Gallery*

Henri Gaudier-Brzeska, 'Red Stone Dancer', *c.*1913, *Tate Gallery*

Wyndham Lewis, 'Red Duet', 1914, *Private Collection*

Edward Wadsworth, 'Abstract Composition', 1915, *Tate Gallery*

Andrea Mantegna, 'The Court', Camera degli Sposi,
Palazzo Ducale, Mantua, 1473–4. Copyright Scala/Firenze

Piero della Francesca, 'Sigismondo Malatesta kneeling before
St Sigismund', Tempio Malatestiano, Rimini, 1451. Copyright Scala/Firenze

Agostino di Duccio, 'Diana', Tempio Malatestiano,
Rimini, 1447–c.1457.
Copyright Scala/Firenze

[31]

Francesco del Cossa, 'April', Palazzo Schifanoia, Ferrara, 1470.
Copyright Scala/Firenze

Demon Pantechnicon Driver:
Pound in the London Vortex, 1908–1920

RICHARD HUMPHREYS

> Cowardly editors threaten: 'If I dare'
> Say this or that, or speak my open mind,
> Say that I hate may [sic] hates,
> Say that I love my friends,
> Say I believe in Lewis, spit out the later Rodin,
> Say that Epstein can carve in stone,
> That Brzeska can use the chisel,
> Or Wadsworth paint;
>   Then they will have my guts . . .[1]

In December 1913 Ezra Pound wrote to his friend, the American poet William Carlos Williams, 'We are getting our little gang after five years of waiting.'[2] Five years earlier, in September 1908, Pound had moved from Venice to London where he lived until his departure for Paris in late 1920. The 'little gang' he referred to was the group of artists and writers associated with the Vorticist movement and its periodical *Blast*, first published in July 1914. The artists with whom Pound was closely associated, or in whom he had a particular interest, were Henri Gaudier-Brzeska, Alvin Langdon Coburn, Jacob Epstein, Wyndham Lewis, Dorothy Shakespear and Edward Wadsworth.

I

Although Pound's first few years in London were dominated by his work as a poet, literary critic and translator, there are many references to the visual arts in his writing of this period.[3] One is constantly aware in reading this material that Pound had a concept, if only half-formed, of literature, painting, sculpture and architecture as intimately linked, and in ways that perhaps had not been considered before. Despite references to Velasquez, the Pre-Raphaelites, Alma-Tadema, Turner, Burne-Jones, Matisse, Goya, the watercolourist William Henry

Hunt, a boyhood friend William Brooke Smith, and oriental art, the artist who stands out most clearly in Pound's thinking, until at least 1912, is James Abbot McNeill Whistler. The American painter had only recently died (in 1903), and had become an heroic figure for Pound. A Browningesque poem written to celebrate the 1912 Whistler retrospective exhibition at the Tate ('that sink of abomination')[4] shows the extent of the young poet's obsession:

> You also, our first great,
> Had tried all ways;
> Tested and pried and worked in many fashions,
> And this much gives me heart to play the game.
>
> Here is part that's slight, and part gone wrong,
> And much of little moment, and some few
> Perfect as Dürer!
> 'In the Studio' and these two portraits if I had my choice!
> And then these sketches in the mood of Greece?
>
> You had your searches, your uncertainties,
> And this is good to know – for us, I mean
> Who bear the brunt of our America
> And try to wrench her impulse into art.
>
> You were not always sure, not always set
> To hiding night or tuning 'symphonies';
> Had not one style from birth, but tried and pried
> And stretched and tampered with the media.
>
> You and Abe Lincoln from that mass of dolts
> Show us there's chance at least of winning through.[5]

In 1909 Pound wrote to his mother about Whistler, comparing the American favourably with J. W. Waterhouse, famous as the painter of 'The Lady of Shalott' (1888).

There are two kinds of artists:
1) Waterhouse who painted perhaps the most beautiful pictures that have ever been made in England; but you go from them and see no more than you did before. The answer is in the picture.
2) Whistler and Turner, to whom it is theoretically necessary to be 'educated up'. When you first see their pictures you say 'wot't– 'ell' but when you leave the picture you see beauty in mists, shadows, a hundred places where you never dreamed of seeing it before. The answer to their work is in nature. The artist is in the maker of an ornament or a key, as he chooses.[6]

J. A. M. Whistler, 'Miss Cicely Alexander', 1872, *Tate Gallery*

Pound's assessment of Whistler, however, was not just an aesthetic one. Whistler represented a 'type' of artist and, like one of Pound's important literary heroes, Henry James, was an American in flight from the constrictions of a philistine culture.

What Whistler has proved, once and for all, is that being born an American does not eternally damn a man or prevent him from the ultimate and highest

[35]

achievements in the arts. And no man before him had proved this. And he proved it over many a hindrance and over many baffled attempts. He is, with Abraham Lincoln, the beginning of our great tradition.[7]

The comparison of Whistler with a politician is of significance, as a letter from Pound to Harriet Monroe of August 1912 underlines:

> Any agonising that tends to hurry what I believe in the end to be inevitable, our American Risorgimento, is dear to me. That awakening will make the Italian Renaissance look like a tempest in a teapot! The force we have, and the impulse, but the guiding sense, the discrimination in applying the force, we must wait and strive for.[8]

These are ambitious words, but they give a strong sense of Pound's motives throughout his career. The 'new age' would bring about a new social and political grammar as well as an aesthetic one.

At a psychological level Pound saw Whistler as a kind of Odyssean dandy and aesthete who had made art his quest and his faith. The artist, in this mythology, is a solitary rebel whose values are in direct opposition to those of the 'crowd'. Pound's own pose as a young poet in Edwardian London was based on the 'enemy' persona Whistler had invented for himself, and the early *Personae* (1909) poems show the extent to which the mask or protective shell was central to Pound's vision. Mirrors abound:

> O Strange face there in the glass!
> O ribald company, o saintly host,
> O sorrow-swept my Fool,
> What answer? O ye myriad
> That strive and play and pass,
> Jest, challenge, counterlie
> I? I? I?
>   And ye?[9]

The language is certainly pre-Imagist and pre-Vorticist but the core-imagery will persist.

These considerations, however, should not conceal the aesthetic importance, for Pound, of Whistler's idea of the autonomy of art. Whistler is referred to constantly as a touchstone of aesthetic excellence. In *Blast* Pound quotes Whistler's dictum, 'You are interested in a certain painting because it is an arrangement of lines and colours.'[10] Pound's most extensive statements about Whistler occur in his book *Gaudier-Brzeska: a Memoir* (1916) where he is drafted in as a posthumous ally of the Vorticists.

Our battle began with Whistler, the delicate, 'classical' Whistler. I believe the
Cerberi of the 'Tate' still consider pre-raphaelitism a violent and dangerous
innovation . . . Whistler was the only man working in England in the
'Eighties' who would have known what we are at and would have backed us
against the mob . . . We return again and again to Pater's 'All arts approach
the conditions of music', and in Whistler's 'Gentle Art' we find sentence after
sentence full of matter –

'Art should be independent of all claptrap, should stand alone and appeal to
artistic sense of eye or ear without confounding this with emotions entirely
foreign to it. The imitator is a poor kind of creature. If the man who paints the
tree, or flower, or other surface he sees before him were an artist, the king of
artists would be the photographer. It is for the artist to do something beyond
this . . . in arrangement of colours to treat a flower as his key, not as his
model.'[11]

Pound goes on to say that although Whistler would have been absolutely in
accord with the aims of the Vorticists, 'we have brought in new keys, and now,
perhaps harsher arrangements.'[12] Nevertheless the root aesthetic is the same, for
'Whistler was the great grammarian of the arts.'[13]

Whistler's importance for Pound was therefore manifold. He presented Pound
with an American hero-figure and a tradition to which he could relate. He took on
the 'vulgar mob' in London and paved the way for a developing rebellion in life and
art. His views on art stressed arrangement of form over imitation and allowed for
close correspondences between music, painting, sculpture and poetry. Whistler,
as an avid orientalist, had, furthermore, been an important link between
European art and that of China and Japan. We shall see later how Pound
developed these ideas in relation to Vorticism and, above all, how important the
oriental connection was.

II

During the years 1908–12 Pound became increasingly involved in the culture of
Edwardian London and moved towards a strong commitment to the 'avant-
garde'. He knew and was admired by W. B. Yeats, and became a close
acquaintance of, among many others, the poet and orientalist Laurence Binyon,
the poets F. S. Flint and Edward Storer, the philosopher T. E. Hulme, the editor of
The New Age, A. R. Orage, for whom Pound later wrote much art criticism, the
novelists Ford Madox Ford and D. H. Lawrence, and the writer and painter
Wyndham Lewis. They all belonged to the predominantly literary milieu of the
Poets' Club, the Secession Club, weekly salons at Mrs Ethel Kibblewhite's in Frith

[37]

Street, Soho, writers' dinners and bookshop meetings. Through Yeats and his future mother-in-law, Olivia Shakespear, Pound became deeply interested in occult studies as well as more conventional philosophy. He took a particular interest, for example, in T. E. Hulme's lectures on Henri Bergson in late 1911. Pound also delivered a long series of lectures on troubadour poets (and others) at the Regent Street Polytechnic which were published in 1910 as *The Spirit of Romance*. Throughout this period he wrote poetry published by Elkin Matthews, whose bookshop in Vigo Street was a favourite haunt of Pound's. He also travelled extensively, making trips to Paris, Italy, Germany and America.[14] There are a few references in his letters to his experiences of the visual arts on these journeys, most notably his trip to see the famous signed column at San Zeno in Verona with Edgar, the architect brother of William Carlos Williams.[15]

In 1912 there was an important development in Pound's activities. By this year, when he was living at 10 Church Walk, Kensington, he became more closely

10 Church Walk, Kensington

involved with younger poets such as T. E. Hulme, the philosopher already mentioned, Richard Aldington, F. S. Flint, Hilda Doolittle and Amy Lowell. Like them, Pound rejected the 'impressionism' and 'symbolism' of the older generation and looked for an entirely new poetic which eventually became known as 'Imagism'. It is as well to dwell on Pound's Imagism for it is an important prelude to Vorticism. His most succinct statement of the Imagists' ideas came in March 1913:

1 Direct treatment of the 'thing', whether subjective or objective.

2 To use absolutely no word that did not contribute to the presentation.

3 As regarding rhythm: to compose in sequence of the musical phrase, not in sequence of a metronome.[16]

Pound explained an 'Image' as 'that which presents an intellectual and emotional complex in an instant of time'.[17] The stress was upon economy and concision of language and a sharpness of perception. 'Don't use such an expression as "dim lands of peace". It dulls the image. It mixes an abstraction with the concrete.'[18] In matters of rhythm and rhyme Pound recommended 'foreign' models – Saxon charms, Hebridean folk says, the verse of Dante and Cavalcanti. This 'use of the past' led Wyndham Lewis to dub Pound a 'demon pantechnicon driver busy with removal of old world into new quarters'.[19] In December 1912 Pound wrote to his parents, 'I've been writing some new stuff in an utterly modern manner.'[20]

The definitive Imagist poem is Pound's 'In a Station of the Metro' based on the Japanese *haiku* (or *hokku*) form:

> The apparition of these faces in the crowd;
> Petals on a wet black bough.[21]

Pound described the composition of this poem in September 1914 in an article on Vorticism:

The 'one-image' poem is a form of super-position, that is to say it is one idea set on top of another. I found it useful in getting out of the impasse in which I had been left by my Metro emotion. I wrote a thirty-line poem, and destroyed it because it was what we call a work of second intensity. Six months later I made a poem half that length

and a year later, Pound recorded, he wrote his *hokku*-like piece.[22] The important aspects of Imagism, then, are its fragmentary nature, its use of oriental models, its avoidance of symbols, excessive use of adjectives and clichéd emotion, its broken rhythm, its interest in 'contemporary' subject matter and, above all, its insistence upon the named concrete object as the basis of the 'image'.

III

'Our thought jumps from the Renaissance to the present because it is only recently that men have begun to combat the Renaissance.'[23] Pound's views on art were greatly influenced by the ideas of T. E. Hulme whose 'Collected Poems', numbering five in all, had been an appendix to Pound's *Ripostes*.[24] Hulme was a rebel and philanderer, a combative, even violent, man, who had once answered Epstein's query as to how long he could tolerate Pound by saying that 'he already knew exactly when he would know to kick him downstairs.'[25] Pound recalled that Hulme's 'evenings' at Mrs Kibblewhite's were 'diluted with crap like Bergson, and it became necessary to use another evening a week if one wanted to discuss our own experiments'.[26] Here Pound was being disingenuous because he was certainly affected by Hulme's version of Bergson's aesthetic theories, and much of what he says about the image as the 'essence of an intuitive language' comes from Bergson. However, despite his translations from and studies of Bergson, Hulme became, in 1913, an exponent of the aesthetic theories of the German writer Wilhelm Worringer.

Worringer's book *Abstraktion und Einfühlung*,[27] published in 1908, set out his idea of 'abstraction' and 'empathy' as opposing principles in art. The empathetic art work, he proposed, was 'organic', imitative and humanist. It was produced by civilisations such as those of Greece and Rome, and the Italian Renaissance, which are individualist, rational and confident. In such cultures men are at ease with the natural world and take pleasure in art forms which embrace it. Abstract art, on the other hand, is inorganic, often non-representational or highly formalised and hieratic. It is predominant in cultures such as the Egyptian, Oceanic and Byzantine, which are despotic, mystical and fearful of the natural world. Such art suggests a 'spiritual' dread of space and asserts itself against nature through geometrical stylisation. The conventions of Western humanist art – modelling, perspective and so on – are absent. Its aim is to fuse 'the natural model with the elements of the purest abstraction, namely geometrical – crystalline regularity, in order by this means to impress upon it the stamp of externalisation and wrest it from temporality and arbitrariness'.[28] Such art had been eclipsed since the Renaissance by the opposing principle of 'empathy'.

Hulme made Worringer's ideas the basis for an attack on Humanism, Romanticism and post-Renaissance Christianity. By the end of 1913 he had written articles on artists such as Epstein, Lewis and Bomberg for *The New Age*. He became the radical critical alternative to the writers Roger Fry and Clive Bell, believing that

so thoroughly are we soaked in the spirit of the period we live in, so strong is its influence over us, that we can only escape from it in an unexpected way, as it were, a side direction like art. [29]

Substituting the terms 'geometric' and 'vital' for Worringer's 'abstraction' and 'empathy' he used his art criticism to 'take on' post-Renaissance Western culture. The new art, like that of Egypt or Byzantium, 'tends to be angular, . . . curves tend to be hard and geometrical . . . the representation of the human body . . . is . . . distorted to fit into stiff lines and cubical shapes of various kinds'. [30] The notion that there was a deep sea-change in Western culture away from the 'soft and vital' art of the previous 500 years could be found in the work of some, mainly British or London-based, contemporary artists. The difference between the old and new geometric art lay in the latter's new source of imagery.

> The new 'tendency towards abstraction' will culminate not so much in the simple geometrical forms found in archaic art, but in the more complicated ones associated in our minds with the idea of machinery. [31]

Engineers' drawings, for instance, with their clean, clear-cut and mechanical shapes were typical of the new style. 'The colour is laid on "mechanically" to demonstrate the form with clarity.' [32] Hulme insisted that modernist art must have 'an organisation, and [be] governed by principles, which are at present exemplified unintentionally, as it were, in machinery'. [33] Behind this aesthetic

T. E. Hulme, c.1916,
photograph by G. C. Beresford

there lay a deep antipathy to science, democracy and humanism – tainted by 'Original Sin', man was not, as Rousseau had believed, perfect, nor was he in harmony with nature. Hulme aspired to a religious transcendence, and art could put man 'into some geometrical shape which lifts him out of the transcience of the organic', could transform the 'organic into something not organic' and 'translate the changing and limited, into something unlimited and necessary'.[34]

The authoritarian tone is obvious – Hulme was an admirer and translator of Georges Sorel whose *Reflections on Violence* was published in 1908.[35] Sorel was anti-democratic and believed it was healthy for working-class violence to be allowed to erupt – men could find new strength through violent action. The connections between art and right-wing politics were being forged during this period and it is no surprise to find men like Lewis and Pound, in their different ways, espousing Fascism after the 1914–18 War. Hulme himself, ironically, was killed at the Front in 1917, as Pound later remembers in Canto XVI.[36] What should not be ignored in considering this 'new' art, its ideology and exponents is that since the Liberal government had come to power in 1906 powerful forces were at work to destabilise the country socially, economically and politically. The question of home rule in Ireland, a series of violent industrial disputes, some inspired by Sorelian 'syndicalists' like Tom Mann, as well as the important issue of female suffrage, in combination led, in 1914, to a state of what one historian has described as near civil war.[37] Whatever their individual attitudes to such a situation might have been, the artists of the 'Pound Era' were undoubtedly affected by its enormity.

Pound's involvement with Hulme, Lewis, Gaudier-Brzeska and others in 1913 and 1914 led eventually to the founding of the Rebel Art Centre, the Vorticist movement and the publication of *Blast*. The atmosphere in the London art world had changed since the Post-Impressionist exhibitions organised by Roger Fry in 1910 and 1912. An even more important introduction to European avant-garde

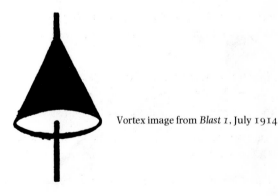

Vortex image from *Blast 1*, July 1914

art, as far as Pound and his colleagues were concerned, was the arrival in London, also in 1910 and 1912, of the Futurist artists, led by the impresario and writer F. T. Marinetti. These developments have been extensively dealt with elsewhere and it is not the aim of this essay to repeat the story.[38] However, Pound was profoundly impressed by the energy of the Futurist movement, as were many others, and was attracted to its aggressive polemicising – William Wees has shown how 'political' the literary and artistic life of London was during these years, with rival factions offering different forms of aesthetic and political radicalism of one degree or another.[39] Pound, like Lewis, enjoyed the cut-and-thrust atmosphere of what he dubbed the 'Vortex' of London. What should be considered now are the main aspects of Pound's Vorticist aesthetic and his pronouncements on those artists most important to him.

IV

The word 'Vorticism' was certainly Pound's invention and came late in the day as a term to distinguish the Rebel Art Centre's work from other 'isms'. Pound used mechanical and scientific imagery to explain the 'Vortex':

> The vortex is the point of maximum energy.
> It represents, in mechanics, the greatest efficiency. We use the words 'greatest efficiency' in the precise sense – as they would be used in a text book of MECHANICS.[40]

Here the quasi-functionalist tone seems indebted to Hulme's ideas about the modern beauty of engineering drawings. Pound, however, is dealing more with mental process or energy and power.

> You may think of man as that toward which perception moves. You may think of him as the TOY of circumstance, as the plastic substance RECEIVING impressions. OR you may think of him as DIRECTING a certain fluid force against circumstance, as CONCEIVING instead of merely observing and reflecting.[41]

There is certainly a Nietzschean ring to these words, but Pound is also alluding to other important sources for the 'Vortex' as he understood it. As early as 1908 he had written a poem, 'Plotinus', which includes the lines

> As one that would draw thru the node of things,
> Back sweeping to the vortex of the cone . . .[42]

William French and Timothy Materer have recently pointed out that the concept of the Vortex was prevalent in Edwardian poetic and occult (particularly Theosophical) circles and that Pound merely appropriated a fashionable term.[43] He was certainly very interested in mystical thought, like most of his contemporaries. Many writers used the 'Vortex' image, for example, Madame Blavatsky, the leader of the Theosophical movement in London ('Blasted' in *Blast* incidentally), who wrote:

> The law of vortical movement in primordial matter, is one of the oldest conceptions of Greek philosophy, whose first historical sages were nearly all Initiates of the Mysteries. The Greeks had it from the Egyptians, and the latter from the Chaldeans, who had been the pupils of Brahmins of the esoteric school.[44]

This kind of writing, searching for a universal religious philosophy, stresses the Vortex as an image of order made out of chaos, of the mind organising form and of a perpetual 'pulse' within the macro- and microcosms. The artist/mystic is the central figure, like a god generating beauty from within himself and out into the world.[45]

Pound sees the Vortex as the shaping receptacle for all experience.

> ALL MOMENTUM, which is the past bearing upon us, RACE, RACE-MEMORY, instinct charging the PLACID, NON-ENERGISED FUTURE. The DESIGN of the future in the grip of the human vortex. All the past that is vital, all the past that is capable of living into the future, is pregnant in the vortex, NOW.[46]

It was during the period when Pound wrote these words that he was also beginning to formulate the idea of his *Cantos* which would include fragments of history as 'significant' or 'luminous' detail, in conjunction with contemporary life, in an attempt to find pattern within history. This sense of the past and of tradition is central to his version of Vorticism and allows him to dismiss Futurism as 'the disgorging spray of a vortex with no drive behind it'.[47] He condemns Futurist painting as an 'accelerated sort of impressionism'.[48]

Having established the ground for the making of art, Pound continues his 'Vortex' by discussing what he termed the 'primary pigment'.

> EVERY CONCEPT, EVERY EMOTION PRESENTS ITSELF TO THE VIVID CONSCIOUSNESS IN SOME PRIMARY FORM. IT BELONGS TO THE ART OF THIS FORM. IF SOUND, TO MUSIC; IF FORMED WORDS, TO LITERATURE; THE IMAGE, TO POETRY; FORM TO DESIGN; COLOUR IN POSITION, TO PAINTING; FORM OR DESIGN IN THREE PLANES, TO SCULPTURE; MOVEMENT TO THE DANCE OR TO THE RHYTHM OF MUSIC OR OF VERSES.[49]

The artist does not try to make his art do what another could do better – each art is autonomous and finds strength and formal coherence in the limitations of its means. This, of course, merely extends Pound's theory of Imagism. Works of 'first intensity' obey the dictates of their own material, works of 'second intensity' imitate and 'disperse'.

In his article on Vorticism already mentioned (see p. 39 above), published in September 1914, Pound makes the connection quite explicit between his earlier formulations for poetry and the more recent ones on painting and sculpture. He writes:

> There is a sort of poetry where music, sheer melody, seems as if it were just bursting into speech. There is another sort of poetry where painting or sculpture seems as if it were "just coming over into speech".[50]

He then reiterates the Imagist theory and asserts a vital inner link between the arts, their particular 'primary pigments' notwithstanding.

> In the 'search' for oneself, in the search for 'sincere self-expression', one gropes, one finds some seeming verity. One says 'I am' this, that, or the other, and with the words scarcely uttered one ceases to be that thing.[51]

Here we return to Pound's Whistlerian masks which, in turn, can be related to the mystic's successive peeling off of layers of the self in the search for an inner core.

Pound uses a mathematical analogy to explain the Vorticist method. He describes arithmetical expression ($2 \times 2 = 4$); algebraic ($a^2 + b^2 = c^2$); geometrical, which realises algebra visually; and 'analytical geometry' which tells us, for example, that $(x - a)^2 + (y - 6)^2 = r^2$ governs all circles.

> In analytics we come upon a new way of dealing with form. It is in this way that art handles life. The difference between art and analytical geometry is the difference of subject matter only. Art is more interesting in proportion as life and the human consciousness are more complex and more interesting than forms and numbers.[52]

V

This last article brings us to a discussion of Pound's first modern 'love' in the visual arts, Henri Gaudier-Brzeska, the young French sculptor killed at the Front in 1915.[53] Pound's meeting with Gaudier-Brzeska (at the Allied Artists exhibition at the Albert Hall in July 1913) coincided with an important moment in his poetic career. Not only was Imagism well under way but Pound had recently become

Yeats's secretary in Sussex.[54] Although his work there concerned Irish myth and folklore he was also becoming interested in Japanese Noh drama and in the writings of Confucius. In October 1913 Pound had met Mary Fenollosa, the widow of the orientalist Ernest Fenollosa. She believed that Pound was the best person to receive her husband's notebooks as he was a practising poet and not an academic. This material included writings on oriental literature, translations of Chinese poetry and Noh plays, and an essay on 'The Chinese Written Character as a Medium for Poetry'. Fenollosa had also written a two-volume book, *Epochs of Chinese and Japanese Art* (1911).[55] Thus began for Pound an obsessive life-long study of the ideogram which complemented his already strong interest in oriental art. Laurence Binyon, who, in 1913, had been put in charge of a new British Museum sub-department of oriental prints and drawings, would have encouraged such an interest. Pound, soon after his arrival in London, had heard a lecture by Binyon on 'Oriental and European Art' which he found 'intensely interesting'.[56] In *Blast 2* Pound quoted Binyon's 1911 essay on oriental art, *The Flight of the*

Henri Gaudier-Brzeska, 1914

Dragon, extensively and approvingly. This was in spite of the fact that he believed Binyon to be too much part of the nineteenth century and insufficiently rebellious. ('Ah well! Mr Binyon has, indubitably, his moments. Very few men do have any moments whatever . . .'[57]) The similarities between Binyon's statements on art and those of Pound are very great. Binyon, for example, is quoted thus: 'Every statue, every picture, is a series of ordered relations, controlled, as the body is controlled in the dance, by the will to express a single idea.' Pound also quotes Binyon on the need for 'rhythmic vitality', the unimportance of representation, the 'signature' of the personality in calligraphy and the correspondence of colours and forms with states of mind.[58] Binyon also insists on the importance of tradition which ensures the 'simultaneous existence' of all art and puts the onus on the artist to 'make it new'.

In his memoir of Gaudier, published in 1916, Pound writes,

he was so accustomed to observe the dominant line in objects that after he had spent, what could not have been more than a few days studying the subject at the museum, he could understand the primitive Chinese ideographs (not the later more sophisticated forms), and he was very much disgusted with the lexicographers who 'hadn't sense enough to see that *that* was a horse,' or a cow or a tree or whatever it might be, 'what the . . . else could it be! The . . . fools!'[59]

The fact that Pound claims the sculptor could read primitive ideograms is important. In the memoir Pound reproduces drawings by Gaudier of a horse in various positions and stages of movement and of a bird, cat, stags, cocks and fledglings. They are described as from a 'Black Note Book' and as being 'progressive studies on the relations of masses'. This phrase underlines their status as studies for sculpture. These are what Pound called 'calligraphic drawings' with pen or brush and ink, and which he preferred to the later 'fine line' drawings. The creatures are reduced to highly stylised strokes which bear close resemblances to Chinese and Japanese ideograms as well as drawing. It seems highly likely that it was Pound who prompted Gaudier to look at oriental art and calligraphy and that he also helped develop the ideas in Gaudier's own 'vortex' statement which Pound claimed would 'become the textbook in all academies of sculpture'.[60] What Gaudier seems to be attempting in these drawings is what Pound believed the ideogram achieved – the capture of the potential energy of a thing in a compressed form. Pound was excited by the possibility of inventing a new language which stressed visual experience and he saw Gaudier's drawings moving in the same direction. Their shared universe was a set of living relations between things perceived by the moving eye and mind. Writing and drawing had their basis in this dynamic universe. As Pound said, 'painting and drawing are first of all

HORSE

PLATE XXXVII

EIGHT LEAVES FROM THE BLACK NOTE BOOK, PROGRESSIVE STUDIES IN THE RELATION OF MASSES
ABOUT ONE-THIRD ORIGINAL DIAMETER

Henri Gaudier-Brzeska, drawings from Pound's 'Memoir', *c.*1914

calligraphy. It is a belief Chinese in origin, or else deduced from Chinese work by some occidental theorist'.[61]

How close poetry and sculpture were for Pound can be seen in his description of a 'pine tree in mist upon the far hill' which 'looks like a fragment of Japanese armour'. The beauty of these two disparate objects, as perceived by the sculptor, lies not in any resemblance they may bear to one another.

> In either case the beauty, in so far as it is beauty of form, is the result of 'planes in relation'. The tree and armour are beautiful because their diverse planes overlie in a certain manner.

The poet

> may cast on the readers' mind a more vivid image of either the armour or the pine by mentioning them close together or by using some device of simile or metaphor . . . for he works not with planes or with colours but with the names of objects and of properties . . . This is the common ground of the arts, this combat of arrangement or 'harmony'.[62]

This unitary thinking is heavily indebted to Ernest Fenollosa whose 'Chinese Written Character' Pound now saw as 'one of the most important essays of our time' which was 'basic for all aesthetics'.[63] Pound made a summary statement about Fenollosa's ideas in his *ABC of Reading*, published in 1934.

> In Europe if you ask a man to define anything, his definition always moves away from the simple things . . . into . . . a region of remoter and progressively remoter abstraction. Thus if you ask him what a red is, he says it is a 'colour'. If you ask him what a colour is, he tells you it is a vibration or a refraction of light, or a division of the spectrum.

Furthermore, the languages of Europe use signs to describe sounds. The Chinese, on the other hand, 'use abbreviated pictures AS pictures, that is to say, Chinese ideogram . . . means the thing or the action or situation, or quality germane to the several things it pictures'.[64] Pound then gives examples of ideograms – 'man' is 人, 'tree' is 木, 'sun' is 日 and 'east' is 東, this last word being a combination of sun and tree to suggest the sun tangled in a tree's branches at sunrise. A more complex or general idea, like 'red' for example, is signified by bringing together the ideograms for a number of known things that are the same colour – 'rose', 'iron rust', 'cherry', 'flamingo'. Although it would not be easy to analyse some of the Vorticist works of Lewis, Gaudier-Brzeska and Wadsworth as actual ideograms there are striking similarities which take their art far beyond being fashionably 'oriental'. The emphasis on clarity, compression and, in some way, capturing an 'essence', are not only close to the canons of classical Chinese art but also to Fenollosa's and

[49]

Henri Gaudier-Brzeska, 'Hieratic Head of Ezra Pound', 1914, *Private Collection*

Pound's concept of the ideogram. Certainly oriental scripts were essential 'keys' for Pound's aesthetic.[65]

When Pound returned to London in early 1914 from his work for Yeats in Sussex the ideas of Vorticism were beginning to cohere. At the time Pound was discovering oriental art, Gaudier began some preliminary drawings, painted in ink with a flat pliable stick in a calligraphic mode, for a large carved pentelicon marble head of the poet. 'In many of them he had undoubtedly no further intention than that of testing a contour,' Pound recalled.[66] Some of these closely resemble the calligraphic drawings already mentioned and in their attempt to create a basic *gestalt* bear witness to Gaudier's assertion, recorded by Pound, that 'it will not look like you, it will . . . not . . . look . . . like you. It will be the expression of certain emotions which I get from your character.'[67] Here we are close to Pound's Imagist and Vorticist idea of an artwork as the direct 'setting down' in tight arrangement of formal 'equivalents' for *feelings*.

The sculpture that resulted is in fact hardly 'Chinese' in character despite its possible feline aspects. It is, as the title tells us, 'hieratic', and indebted for its monumental, indeed phallic, form to the gigantic Easter Island figure, Hoa-Haka-Nana-la, which Gaudier had studied at the British Museum.[68] The totemic and phallic aspects of the 'Hieratic Head' are deliberate ingredients and remind us of an important literary figure whom Pound was beginning to admire – Allen Upward, who had himself, in an essay *The New Word*, considered the linguistic applications of the vortex image.[69] Pound was a fervent admirer of Upward's *The Divine Mystery* which had dealt with the ideas of the witch doctor, leader and artist/genius and their anthropological origins. Upward had also provided Pound, the 'Pagan', with 'Scientific' arguments that could be used against 'the buncomb' of Christianity. The world was full of invisible 'forces' to which the genius, like the primitive witch doctor, is sensitive. Discussing a Nigerian 'lord of thunder' whose ritual dance in a wizard's robe had brought thunder, Upward explained that

> he was more quick than other men to feel the changes of the atmosphere;
> perhaps he had rendered his nervous system more sensitive still by fasting or
> mental abstraction; and he had learned to read his own symptoms as we read
> a barometer. So, when he felt the storm gathering about his head, he put on
> his symbolical vestment and marched forth to be its word, the archetype of all
> Heroes in all Mysteries.[70]

This closely corresponds to Pound's view of the poet as the 'antennae of the race' and to the image of the artist as the still centre of the vortex which whirls about him and which he orders. This impassive seer was what Gaudier was trying to embody in the asymmetric 'arrangement of planes' in his sculpture: 'There is in the final condition of the stone a great calm,' he believed, as well as an image of the virile fertility god.[71]

Pound wrote a number of appraisals of Gaudier's sculpture, concentrating his attention on a few, for him, crucial pieces. An important early work was 'The Dancer',

> in a French or even Parisian style, not in the least revolutionary, but interesting as showing Gaudier's very early interest in the crook'd-arm angle. Note that this form stays with the sculptor and is again in use after any number of revolutions of style, in the 'Red Stone Dancer'.[72] (colour plate, p.26)

The latter work was a transitional piece which, perhaps unhappily, brought geometrical emphasis to a sinuous 'organic' work – as if Hulme's vital and geometric styles were locked in a fight. Pound gives an extended description of the piece.

> This . . . is almost a thesis of Gaudier's ideas upon the use of pure form. We have the triangle and the circle asserted, *labled* [sic] almost, upon the face and right breast. Into these so-called 'abstractions' life flows, the circle moves and elongates into the oval, it increases and takes volume in the sphere or hemisphere of the breast. The triangle moves toward organism, it becomes a spherical triangle (the central life-form common to both Brzeska and Lewis). These two developed motifs work as themes in a figure. We have the whole series of spherical triangles, as in the arm over the head, all combining and culminating in the great sweep of the back of the shoulders, as fine as any surface in all sculpture. The 'abstract' or mathematical bareness of the triangle and circle are fully incarnate, made flesh, full of vitality and of energy. The whole form-series ends, passes into stages with the circular base or platform.[73]

Other works by Gaudier which were important for Pound included three he owned, 'Boy with Coney', 'Cat', and 'Fawn Crouching', as well as the highly stylised 'Birds Erect', which Pound described as

> one of the most important pieces. The representative element is very slight. The work is the culmination of the study of a set of forms begun in Mr Hulme's toy . . . There forms are in some degree related to the series of forms used in the 'Bird Swallowing a Fish', but they are distinctly different. As a composition of masses I do not think I have seen any modern sculpture to match it.[74]

'Boy with Coney' is compared by Pound with Epstein's 'Sun God' and his own poem 'The Return' which evokes the 'powers' of the past as they emerge into the present:

> See, they return; ah, see the tentative
> Movements, and the slow feet,
> The trouble in the pace and the uncertain
> Wavering![75]

As with Gaudier's long statement in *Blast*, Pound's poem is concerned with the 'usable past'.

The Gaudier 'myth' was very largely Pound's invention. 'The vivid, incisive manner, the eyes "almost alarmingly intelligent" . . . His stillness seemed an action, such was the daemon of energy that possessed him, or served him.'[76] There would never be another Gaudier who could tell one 'the whole history of Poland in half an hour, with a sketch of the constitution'.[77] Working in poverty, he used fragments from monument-cutters' yards and 'saw' in these forlorn pieces the shapes of animals and human bodies and faces. He made his own tools at a forge, taking a whole day to temper his chisels made from old steel spindles. 'He liked to do the "whole thing" from start to finish; to feel as independent as the savage.'[78] He even cut metal direct and carved a toothbrush.

One of the images Pound is keenest to record is Gaudier's studio in Putney, under the railway arch. During the cutting of the 'Hieratic Head' Pound sat on a 'shilling wooden chair in a not over-heated studio with the railroad trains rushing overhead'.[79] One day Gaudier slept in the studio 'and woke up to find himself

Horace Brodzky, Interior of Gaudier-Brzeska's Studio, Putney, 1915
Tate Gallery

[53]

inundated with rain and lying in several inches of water'.[80] Despite his working
conditions and lack of money Gaudier made drawings and sculpture which Pound
saw as among the finest achievements of the 'Renaissance' he believed was taking
place. Pound's only fear for his little sculptor was that the rigours of his life at the
front would 'soften' him and weaken his resolve so that his art would 'react into
Condor, the nineties, delicate shades and half-lights'.[81] Gaudier, killed on 5 June
1915, was unable to prove him wrong.

VI

Last evening I watched a friend's parrot outlined against a hard grey-silver
twilight. That is a stupid way of saying that I had found a new detail or a new
co-relation with Mr Epstein's stone birds. I saw anew that something
masterful had been done. I got a closer idea of a particular kind of decision.[82]

Jacob Epstein, an expatriate American, was the other sculptor in London whom
Pound championed. At one point, in fact, he was 'the only sculptor in England'.[83]
'The sculptors of England, with the exception of Epstein, are, or were until the
beginning of the war, we suppose, engaged wholly in making gas-fittings and
ornaments for electric light globes, etc.,'[84] Pound complained in 1915, bemoan-
ing the public ignorance of Epstein's work. The public still desire the Hellenic and
'caressable', unaware that if that is their desire then real silk and flesh are
preferable to marble or bronze.

We hold that life has its own satisfactions, and that after a man has lived life
up to the hilt, he should still have sufficient energy to go on to the satisfactions of art, which are different from the satisfactions of life . . . The result of
the attempt to mix the satisfactions of art and life is, naturally, muddle . . . for
example the drawings in salacious 'comics' or the domesticities of Pears'
Annual – the Mecca of British Academicians.[85]

The clear-cut distinction between 'art' and 'life' was central to the Vorticist
doctrine.

Pound wrote in 1915: 'So far as I am concerned, Jacob Epstein was the first
person who came talking about "form, not the form of anything". It may have
been Mr T. E. Hulme, quoting Epstein.'[86] Hulme had been Epstein's major defender
in 1913 and 1914 and Epstein was the artist, along with David Bomberg, who
most satisfactorily carried out his demands for a geometrical art. Hulme, however,
was never entirely happy with Epstein's primitivism and urged the sculptor to
consider the possibilities of mechanical form. This led to Epstein's 'Rock-Drill'

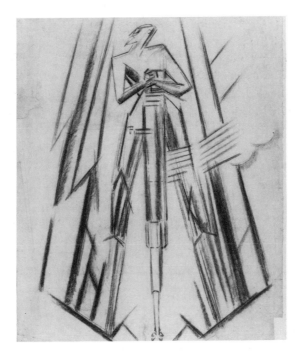

Jacob Epstein, Study for 'Rock Drill', 1913
Tate Gallery

sculpture, one of the most dramatic, perhaps melodramatic, of all Vorticist images.

For Pound such questions were of less importance than Epstein's status as a carver and his truth to materials.

> Epstein is a 'slow worker', perhaps. His mind works with the deliberation of the chisel driving through stone, perhaps. The work is conceived from the beginning, slow stroke by slow stroke, like some prehistoric age-long upheaval in natural things, driven by natural forces . . . full of certitude and implacable and unswerving . . . perhaps.[87]

Pound is implicitly comparing Epstein's mature slowness with Gaudier's youthful mercuriality. This passage is in fact very close to Gaudier's appraisal of the 'artisan' values typified by Brancusi where 'every inch is won at the point of a chisel – every stroke of the hammer is a physical and mental effort'.[88] Carving as a mode was given almost complete priority over modelling and Pound's convictions about this remained with him for the rest of his career. The carver has to respond with skill and sensitivity to his block – there are no second chances, as there are

[55]

Jacob Epstein, 'Doves', *c.*1913, *Tate Gallery*

with modelling, and the stone imposes a form on the sculptor's wishes. Discussing 'Doves' and other pieces Pound writes,

> These things are great art because they are sufficient in themselves . . . Representing, as they do, the immutable, the calm thoroughness of unchanging relations, they are as the gods of the Epicureans, apart, unconcerned, unrelenting.[89]

Pound, typically, affects a certain inarticulateness about his response to Epstein's work. The 'theory' was safer to deal with than an empirical response.

> Art is to be admired rather than explained. The jargon of these sculptors is beyond me. I do not precisely know why I admire a green granite, female, apparently pregnant monster with one eye going round a square corner.[90]

Pound avoids a formal description in favour of a literary one, elsewhere despised. 'The green flenite woman expresses all the tragedy and enigma of the germinal universe: she is also permanent, unescaping.'[91] (colour plate, p.25) A salient example for Pound of a sculptor who inclines to 'telling a story' is the Yugoslav

Ivan Mestrovic who was working in various parts of Europe during the war. Pound asks us to note by contrast 'how utterly absent the narrative element is from Epstein's flenites'. Mestrovic, who has 'the milkman's itch to be the eighty-third Michelangelo', is also used as an example of a sculptor who has no feeling for stone or form and who makes up for his deficiencies by indulging in 'a weakly barbaric symbology'. Pound observes with cruelty that when a 'man's mind is so fundamentally uninteresting and uninventive as the mind displayed by Mr Mestrovic in his sculpture, he would do well . . . to stick to the matter of his craft'.[92]

VII

It was Epstein who told Pound that Lewis's drawings had the quality of sculpture. 'That', said Pound, 'set me off looking at Lewis'.[93] Pound's relationship with Wyndham Lewis was complex and lasted with interruptions until the latter's death in 1957. Lewis, like Gaudier, made portraits of Pound and although he was often critical of the American's art and personality he was evidently fond of him. The 1939 portrait shows Pound as a dreaming feline creature lost in a world of, perhaps, atavistic fantasy. This is in marked distinction to the earlier 'heroic' portrait in which, as Pound wrote, the poet 'rises with the dignity of a classic stele to the god of gardens amid the bundles of garden produce'.[94] Perhaps the most important aspect of Pound's interest in Lewis as a visual artist was that the editor of *Blast* was a writer as well. There was, so to speak, a tougher intellect for Pound to deal with. As Pound wrote in 1919, Lewis 'is needless to say our most searching

Wyndham Lewis, *c.*1912, *Barratt's Photo Press*

[57]

and active art critic . . . since Whistler's "Ten O'Clock" no man actually a painter has been able to present thought about painting'.[95]

> Mr Wyndham Lewis is one of the greatest masters of design yet born in the occident. Mr Lewis has in his 'Timon' gathered together his age . . . The 'man in the street' cannot be expected to understand the Timon at first sight. Damn the man in the street, once and for all, damn the man in the street who is only in the street because he hasn't intelligence enough to be let in to anywhere else . . .[96]

The belligerent tone, which from 1914 is Pound's distinctive trademark, is suitable for the works to which Pound is referring. Lewis's portfolio of drawings for Shakespeare's *Timon of Athens* was the work Pound cited most frequently when insisting on Lewis's greatness. Timon's misanthropic rejection of a materialistic society was an ideal expression of both poet's and artist's defiance of Edwardian vulgarity. Timon, wrote Pound, is the embodiment of 'the sullen fury of intelligence baffled, shut in by the entrenched forces of stupidity'.[97] Pound invokes the 'creative principle' of the vortex to emphasise Lewis's power with an apparent allusion to the sexual/mechanical imagery of Epstein's 'Rock-Drill'. 'The intelligent god is incarnate in the universe, in struggle with the endless inertia . . . the struggle of driving the shaft of intelligence into the dull mass of mankind'.[98] The 'emotional geometry' of the work is that of 'a man at war' and 'if he have made "Timon" a type emotion and delivered it in lines and masses and planes, it is proper that we should respect him in a way that we do not respect men blaring out truisms or doing an endless embroidery of sentiment.'[99] Timon, as far as Pound was concerned, was Lewis, and perhaps anticipates his own Malatesta. Pound at times seems overwhelmed by Lewis, though as a promoter he would make every effort to paint his protégé large. He wrote enthusiastically to the financial lawyer and patron of art and letters, John Quinn,

> The vitality, the fullness of the man . . . Nobody has any conception of the volume and energy and the variety . . . It is not merely knowledge of technique, or skill, it is intelligence and knowledge of life, of the whole of it, beauty, heaven, hell, sarcasm, every kind of whirlwind of force and emotion. Vortex. That is the right word, if I did find it myself. Every kind of geyser from jism bursting up white as ivory, to hate or a storm at sea. Spermatozoon, enough to repopulate the island with active and vigorous animals. Wit, satire, tragedy.[100]

As with Gaudier, Pound finds in Lewis's art the unmistakable oriental touch.

I have here also the design out of 'Timon', marked Act III, and a Japanese

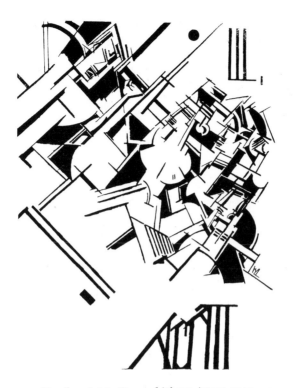

Wyndham Lewis, Timon of Athens, Act III, 1912

print which is curiously cubist. Plenty of people admire the latter and I am at a loss to know why they cannot admire the former. I have also another 'full-sheet' black and white design out of the 'Timon', the one with the big circular arrow, and that seems to me the strongest of them all, the one that has most moved me to this rhapsody.[101]

In a letter to John Quinn, switching his 'orient' somewhat, Pound asserts, 'if any man is to bring into Western art the power of Chinese painting it will be Lewis.'[102] Lewis, 'the genius of the protoplasm',[103] becomes a kind of modernist Whistler in his

deliberate search into ugly colour . . . I think . . . that Lewis with his fundamental realism has been trying to show the beauty of the colour one actually sees in a modern brick, iron, sooty, rail road yarded smoked modern city. I think his revelation, or his training of the beholder or whatever we are to call it, is very largely in an investigation of drab colours which are ordinarily looked away from in so far as it has to do with colour at all.[104]

[59]

Wyndham Lewis, 'Workshop', 1914–15, *Tate Gallery*

Whereas Whistler invented a London of atmospheric mists and Japanese charm, Lewis, in works like 'Workshop', bought by Quinn, is the discoverer of beauty in the 'ugly'. He is '*the* inventor. THE organiser of forms, at the present moment. *The* fecund mind with any amount of form-organisation fermenting in it.'[105] Pound asked Quinn to consider Lewis's abilities in relation to Stuart Davis whom Quinn was collecting.

> I haven't seen Davies [sic] things, and can therefore make no sensible comparison. There is a deal of force in the 'Kermess'. I wonder has Davies the perception of humanity (literary talent?) which keeps leaking into Lewis painting, or rather drawing?[106]

This repeats, with reference to an individual, the famous image of the magnet Pound used in 1915.

> For example: if you clap a strong magnet beneath a plateful of iron filings, the energies of the magnet will proceed to organise form. It is only by applying a particular and suitable force that you can bring order and vitality and thence beauty into a plate of iron filings, which are otherwise as 'ugly' as anything under heaven. The design in the magnetised iron filings expresses a confluence of energy.[107]

[60]

Pound compares this virile force with the 'charming' (feminine) automatic drawings of Miss Florence Seth which purport to be made without preconception, guided by 'spirits'. This symbolist, mediumistic work has the structure of leaves and viscera. It is 'organic' and achieved in a state of passivity. 'This is not vorticism . . .' and the work 'is interesting as a psychological problem, not as creation'.[108] The subconscious urge is present, as it should be, but such automatism cannot express the 'will and consciousness' of the Vortex. Pound echoed Lewis's own strictures about the lack of 'structure' in Kandinsky's early abstract work and was sensitive to Lewis's desire in *Blast* to have nothing 'soft' or impressionistic. Pound's attempt to achieve a 'sense of form' in a Vorticist poem was his 'Dogmatic Statement on the Game and Play of Chess – Theme for a Series of Pictures', which he later said showed 'the effect of modern abstract art':

> Red knights, brown bishops, bright queens
> Striking the board, falling in strong 'L's' of colour,
> Reaching and striking in angles,
>   Holding lines of one colour:
> This board is alive with light

Wyndham Lewis, 'Vorticist Composition'
1915, *Tate Gallery*

[61]

> These pieces are living in form,
>> Their moves break and reform the pattern:
> Luminous greens from the rooks,
>> Clashing with 'x's' of queens,
>> Looped with the knight-leaps.
> 'Y' pawns, cleaving, embanking,
> Whirl, centripetal, mate, king down in the vortex:
> Clash, leaping of bands, straight strips of hard colour,
> Blocked lights working in, escapes, renewing of contest.[109]

This was no doubt a response to the extraordinary prose of Lewis's *Enemy of the Stars* published in the first issue of *Blast*. Lewis had written this 'play', he claimed, to show what could be done with a 'Vorticist' prose. Even though Pound had earlier written two lines deriding the delicacies of Post-Impressionist painting,

> Green arsenic smeared on an egg-white cloth,
> Crushed strawberries! Come, let us feast our eyes,[110]

he must also have felt his own writing to lack the hardness and compression of Lewis's painting and prose. He was eventually to realise that aggressive description was a simplistic, or at least very incomplete, response to the problems posed for poetry by his own multifarious interests. 'Dogmatic statement' falls into the trap of trying to achieve in one art what can be achieved best in another – It could not compete, for instance, with Lewis's 'Red Duet' of 1914. (colour plate, p.27)

VIII

The other Vorticist painter who seriously interested Pound was Edward Wadsworth. Pound, as usual, defines Wadsworth's art in terms of his personality and its differences from, in this instance, Lewis's. Lewis is 'a restless, turbulent intelligence . . . full of sudden, illuminating antipathies . . .' Wadsworth is gentler, more stable and limited. 'I cannot recall any painting of Mr Wadsworth's where he seems to be angry.'[111] Possibly more than Lewis's work, the cool, workmanlike woodcuts of Wadsworth were the modernist transformations of oriental art which were most convincing, though by no means the most 'vigorous'. 'Mr Wadsworth has given us . . . woodcuts which afford interesting comparison with the work of Japanese woodcuts.'[112] The Wadsworth version of Vorticism has 'cleanliness, efficiency, precision'.[113] His art lacks the emotional grandeur, the Nietzschean complexity of Lewis, but gains points in its clinical subtlety. It takes 'delight in ports and harbours and in the vernal processes of nature; as . . . even his

Edward Wadsworth, 'Harbour of Flushing', *c.*1914

machinery [tends] toward an oriental angular grace . . . From Whistler and the Japanese, or Chinese, the "world" . . . learned to enjoy "arrangements" of colours and masses.' Pound is insistent on this quality he perceives in Wadsworth's art and takes the 'aesthetic' line that the pictures do 'not "look like" anything, save perhaps a Chinese or Japanese painting'.[114] The relationship between the woodcuts and oriental art is seen by Pound (as he had discovered in Gaudier's drawings) to be based on the ideogram.

> These woodcuts make interesting comparison with the Chinese work. There
> [China] they have their traditional radicals from which each picture develops
> ie. their ideograph for bamboo or for willow. Here we must find a language.[115]

Pound finds in the woodcuts precise demonstrations of his beliefs. 'I think the harbour is admirable. The mist and sails, ideograph. And the splendid organisation. Also the *Rotterdam* (or some Dutch town).'[116] The oriental aesthetic was, for Pound, founded upon 'form' which 'informs' the perceptions and gives life coherence.

> It is possible that this search for form-motif will lead us to some synthesis of
> western life comparable to the synthesis of oriental life which we find in
> Chinese and Japanese painting. This lies with the future. Perhaps there is
> some adumbration of it in Mr Wadsworth's 'Harbour of Flushing'.[117]

Wadsworth's dense compressions of views of towns, harbours and the like are 'keys' to further apperceptions. With them the spectator has a 'musical conception' of form and this can be used

> to select motives of form from the forms before you, that you can recombine
> and recolour them and 'organise' them into new form – this conception, this
> state of mental activity, brings with it a great joy and refreshment . . . It is one
> of the simple pleasures of those who have no money to spend on joy-rides and
> on suppers at the Ritz.[118]

The musical analogy, taken partly from Whistler of course, is used most persistently when Pound writes about Wadsworth. This is particularly appropriate as Wadsworth had translated passages from Kandinsky's *Uber das Geistige in der Kunst* (1912) for *Blast 1*. Kandinsky's book had placed a great deal of emphasis upon the musical aspects of art and had distinguished between simple and 'melodic' compositions, predominantly Western, and complex 'symphonic' composition which was mostly typical of oriental art. Wadsworth quotes this and also Kandinsky's statement, 'FORM IS THEN THE UTTERANCES OF ITS INNER CONTENT'.[119] Kandinsky's influence on Pound's thinking in 1914 was obviously considerable and may even have affected his poetry. Complex symphonic

[64]

Edward Wadsworth, 'View of a Town', *c.*1918, *Tate Gallery*

composition was as much the aim of *The Cantos* as it was of Lewis's or Wadsworth's Vorticist art.

In his 'authorised appreciation' of Wadsworth's art, Pound wrote:

There is a definite, one might say a musical or a music-like pleasure for the eye in noting the arrangement of the very acute angles combined like 'notes in a figure' in this drawing of Mr Wadsworth's. One is much more at ease in comparing this new work to music. I recall a black and white of Mr Wadsworth's, a thing like a signal arm or some other graceful unexplained bit of machinery, reaching out, and alone, across the picture, like a Mozart theme skipping an octave, or leaving the base for the treble.[120]

In 1915, in an essay on the musician Arnold Dolmetsch, Pound states his own preference for 'pattern music' (as in Bach's fugues) over 'impressionistic, emotional' music of the Wagnerian and nineteenth-century kind. 'Pattern music' is then compared with Vorticist painting.[121] This again reminds us that Pound's thinking has a consistent strand of mysticism and neo-platonism running through it. At the end of his Gaudier *Memoir* Pound refers to John Heydon, the seventeenth-century neo-Platonist, who, 'long before our present day theorists, had written of the joys of pure form . . . inorganic, geometrical form, in his "Holy Guide"'.[122] Heydon's work of 1662, borrowed by Pound from Mrs Yeats, explains the love of geometrical natural objects as a reflection of the needs of our soul.

> These stones (round or regularly angular), I say, gratify our sight as having a nearer cognation with the soul of man that is rational and intellectual, and therefore is well pleased when it meets with any other outward object that fits and agrees with these congenite ideas her own nature is furnished with.[123]

IX

With the outbreak of the war Pound's art activities changed and perhaps increased. With many artists at the Front and the London artistic and literary world a ghost of its former self, he diverted his energies into proselytising the new art, finding patrons for it, finding publishers for avant-garde literature such as Lewis's novel *Tarr*, deepening his oriental studies and, by the end of 1915, working seriously on the first *Cantos*. Of his frenetic activity, particularly on behalf of the others, he wrote, 'I have never been so rushed. I seem to be a universal committee "for the arts".'[124] Pound contributed poems and notes to *Blast 2* in July 1915 and also gave an interview to Zinaida A. Vengerova for the Russian Futurist miscellany *Strelets* (The Archer) which was published in St Petersburg in January or February 1915. Pound had probably met Vengerova some time before this and listed her as a prospective faculty member of the College of Arts in November 1914. He seems, in the interview, to be trying to emulate Marinetti who had visited Russia in early 1914 on a promotion tour for Italian Futurism. In the interview, which he probably never saw, Pound was adamant about the independence of the Vorticists from other movements. The piece begins:

> 'English Futurists. . .'
> 'No, we are not futurists, above all, not futurists,' I am interrupted, with
> malevolent determination, by a tall, slender, blond young man who wears his
> long hair combed backward, and who has an angular cast of countenance, a
> large nose, and penetrating, never smiling eyes. . .

His persona established, Pound defined the vortex as

that point in the cyclone where energy cuts into space and imparts form to it
... We are the vortex in the heart of the present; and the pattern of angles and
geometric lines which is formed by our vortex in the existing chaos, in life and
in culture, is the crux of our art.

Although *Strelets* also reproduced Lewis's *Portrait of an Englishwoman*, Vengerova
and, it would seem, most of the rest of Russia, were not particularly impressed by
Pound's beliefs. As he was to find elsewhere, Vorticism did not have the impact he
and his colleagues hoped for.[125]

Pound's attention also turned towards broader cultural and political matters,
presaging his 'conversion' to Major Douglas's theories of 'social credit' in the
1920s. In his article 'Analysis of the Decade', Pound took the Italian Renaissance
as the epoch most suitable for comparison with his own times. 'It may be an
hallucination but one seems able to find modern civilisation in its simple elements
in the Renaissance.'[126] There had never been a period in which the arts and
'power' were so intermingled and Pound saw it as a golden age. He gave a potted
list of 'forces' which made the Renaissance – 'an exhilarating hotchpotch' which
nevertheless,

in the midst of these awakenings . . . went to rot, destroyed by rhetoric,
destroyed by the periodic sentence and by the flowing paragraph . . . For when
words cease to cling close to things, kingdoms fall, empires wane and
diminish . . . The rhetoric got into painting. The habit of having no definite
convictions, that it was glorious to reflect life in a given determined costume
or decoration 'did for' the painters.[127]

Pound then jumped ahead to the present: it was only at this time that this flaccid
Renaissance culture was being combated – not by 'pious catholicism' or 'limited
medievalism' but by a 'new focus'. He listed the 'simple ideas' of the decade as: 'a
sense of the mot juste', of the 'need for a uniform criticism of excellence', of the
'image', of emotion in abstract design, of 'the feeling of masses in relation', of the
need of 'radicals in design', of the beauty of machinery, of the value of the 'creative,
constructive individual', of the importance of China.

And this force of external stimuli is certainly not limited by 'what we do';
these new masses of unexplored arts and facts are pouring into the vortex of
London. They cannot help but bring about changes as great as the
Renaissance changes.[128]

The interest in the Italian Renaissance as a period of intense patronage, in
which financial and political power gave the arts a tremendous impetus, found its
way in the 1920s into *The Cantos* in the shape of the despot of Rimini, Sigismundo

John Quinn

Malatesta, who built the Tempio Malatestiano. In his own day, though, Pound was looking for wealthy patronage. The man who, at least during the war, became for Pound what W. B. Yeats called 'the nearest approach to an angel in my experience',[129] was John Quinn. Pound had met Quinn in New York in 1910 but then lost contact with him until 1915 when a boisterous article by Pound attacking the want of interest in modern art among American collectors elicited a response from the lawyer. 'If there is a "liver" collector of vital contemporary art in this country, for a man of moderate means, I should like to meet him,' he wrote to Pound, mentioning that he had already six pieces by Epstein and that he would be interested to see work by Gaudier.[130] Pound replied, giving a 'character' of the ideal patron,

> My whole drive is that if a patron buys from an artist who needs money
> (needs money to buy tools, time and food), the patron then makes himself
> equal to the artist: he is building art into the world; he creates . . . A great age
> of painting, a renaissance in the arts, comes when there are a few patrons
> who back their own flair and who buy from unrecognised men.[131]

This began a series of transactions between the men in which the poet propagandised for the Vorticists, dealt with shipping, insurance and payment, and suggested which works were most appropriate. With regard to the choice of works Pound could be very dogmatic, telling Quinn of the different versions of Epstein's 'Doves', 'for God's sake get the two that are stuck together, not the pair in which one is standing up on its legs'.[132] Quinn wrote to Epstein about this, and although the sculptor agreed with the choice, he wanted to know who Pound thought he was to make it. On a different matter, when Pound cabled Quinn at the end of 1915 with the news that Lewis was enlisted and needed money because of his debts, £30 was immediately cabled to the artist. After Gaudier's death Quinn promised to buy as much of his work as possible and to underwrite a Vorticist exhibition in New York. Neither enterprise ran smoothly. The negotiations with Sophie Brzeska were difficult because of her fear of shipping works through submarine-infested waters, and Quinn felt wounded by her apparent suspiciousness of him. The same difficult lady almost prevented the Vorticist exhibition from going ahead when she refused to allow Gaudier's work to be shown in it. Quinn told Pound that if this were the case then the show should be cancelled. Pound wrote back, 'Ma che Cristo about the Vorticist show!!! I simply can't stop it now. The boys have sent in the stuff, and if I don't go I can never look anybody in the face again.'[133] Further problems ensued and when the exhibition, at the Penguin Club in January 1917, was put on it was not a success. Pound's big effort to take the 'Renaissance' to New York, a cherished dream, had failed despite Quinn's purchase of works by Etchells, Lewis, Roberts and Wadsworth.

X

Pound's major 'discovery' in the visual arts during the war, mentioned in a letter to Quinn in 1917, was the photography of Alvin Langdon Coburn. Coburn, another expatriate American, had taken Pound's portrait in 1913 which had been used, for its 'seductive and sinister' qualities, as the frontispiece for the *Lustra* poems in 1916.[134] He had also become fascinated by the possibility of an 'abstract' photography through his contact with the Vorticists, and, in turn, his own dramatic images of New York and other major cities seem to have influenced some of Lewis's and Wadsworth's work. Like Pound, Coburn was deeply interested in oriental art and occult ideas and it seems likely that both he and Pound saw in 'vortography' a formal language that also spoke of 'secret things'. Certainly in their similarities to Wadsworth's work the vortographs are attempts at 'radicals of design', Pound's banner headline for them being 'THE CAMERA IS FREED FROM REALITY'. Towards the end of 1916, according to Pound, Coburn invented the 'vortoscope', using bits of broken glass from Pound's old shaving mirror 'fastened

Alvin Langdon Coburn, Vortograph of Ezra Pound, 1916–17

together in the form of a triangle, and resembling to a certain extent the Kaleidoscope . . . The mirrors acted as a prism splitting the image formed by the lens into segments.'[135] The two men worked quite closely together during the winter of 1916–17, and an exhibition of vortographs was held at the Camera Club in London in February 1917. The 'vortographs' of Pound himself are varied. 'The Centre of the Vortex' is closer to Futurist photography in that movement is suggested by concentric images of the poet, while other vortographs are more abstract and geometric, incorporating Pound's profile into an overall design. A number of vortographs were also made by arranging objects like crystals and pieces of wood on a glass table. The abstracted patterns were usually blurred to remove a sense of the objects' specificity.

Pound attempted a definition of the 'primary pigment' of vortography.

> The medium of the vortographer is practically limited in form (shapes on a surface) and to light and shade; to the peculiar varieties in lightness and darkness which belong to the technique of the camera.

However, he believed that vortography could never rival the other Vorticist arts because it is an 'art of the eye, not of the eye and hand together. It stands infinitely above photography in that the vortographer combines his forms at *will*.'[136]

Alvin Langdon Coburn, Vortograph, 1917

Although these views annoyed Coburn and the two argued about it, Pound placed a lot of faith in the photographer's work – after all, in 1916 and 1917 virtually nothing was being produced by the other Vorticists – and he voiced a hope that its experiments might be fruitful for painting and sculpture.

> Certain definite problems in the aesthetics of form may possibly be worked out with the vortoscope. When these problems are solved vorticism will have entered that phase of morbidity into which representative painting descended after the Renaissance painters had decided upon all the correct proportions of the human body, etc., etc., etc., That date of decline is still far off.[137]

Partly due to their disagreements over the worth of photography and partly because Coburn got bored with vortography the whole enterprise was shortlived.

XI

Writing under the pseudonym 'B. H. Dias', Pound, needing to supplement his meagre income, reviewed art exhibitions extensively for *The New Age* between 1917 and 1919. His 'Art Notes' deal not only with the works of Vorticists and other modernists but with more academic artists. In certain cases he is passionately jocular: 'The Royal Academy, oh God, the Royal Academy! The Royal Academy is, before God, nothing to joke about.'[138] In other instances he is completely dismissive:

> The Orpen Show need not detain one – Slade, Slade Sketch Club, Society tinted-photos . . . Sir William's message is that the war is very like peace-life in Belgravia – bright cheery tints, lemonish egg-yolk yellow. Any tone of war, any feeling of war, wholly absent . . . Ease, comfort, complexion soap, a little stage decoration. A pale cast of prettiness.[139]

This should be compared with Pound's response to Lewis's war art where

> there is definite proof of anatomic skill in the degree of tenseness in the various figures . . . and this expression or exposure of bodily capability as shown by the artist with the fine graduation of a master.[140]

There are also reviews and opinions on portrait busts by Epstein, and works by Matisse, William Nicholson, Paul Nash, Augustus John, C. R. W. Nevinson; exhibitions at Heal's, the Leicester, Grafton and Alpine Club Galleries, the New English Art Club, the Pastel Society, the National Portrait Society, the Royal Institute of Painters in Watercolour and the Allied Artists' Association; an assessment of photography which is 'poor art because it has to put in everything, or nearly everything', Pound writes, no doubt referring to vortography, which 'omits by a general blur'; the (silent) cinema, 'an excellent medium for news' and education and which is the 'phonograph of appearance'; a brief consideration of the 'functions of criticism' and a eulogy to the collection of the late Captain Guy Baker which, as with Pound's comments to Quinn, asserts the 'creative' aspect of adventurous patronage. This extensive reviewing shows Pound to have been a conscientious traveller around the London galleries and a fairly thorough observer of the contents of exhibitions. He was, in fact, surprisingly sympathetic to utterly non-Vorticist artists like Fred Brown, the Slade professor, and Charles Ricketts, 'a very talented archaeologist, and possessed of genius for water colour'.[141]

The most interesting development in Pound's criticism at this time, however, is an increasing concern with architecture. 'The aesthetic of the architectural is the least explored aesthetic of our time.'[142] It was just after this period that Etchells turned towards architecture and that Lewis and Wadsworth became aware of the importance of painting's relationship to building and design. All of these London-based artists, and Pound himself, were attuned to the growth of the 'modern movement' in Europe – Purism, De Stijl, Constructivism and so on. In his writing on architecture for *The New Age*, Pound takes the reader (the previously maligned 'man-in-the-street') on a 'walk-about' of 'miles of abominable street' in London, assessing eighteenth-, nineteenth- and twentieth-century building from the 'front' only. Mostly, says Pound, a walk through London produces 'an almost uninterrupted series of rather acute disgusts', which in the case of Ruskin led to insanity![143] The beauties of London building are her Georgian houses – the rot sets in after 1850. 'The horror of London is its grey-yellow brick . . . In the more pretentious houses there is added to this the horror of machine-cast stone trimmings.'[144] Such ornament, or 'excrescence', is a mendacity as it tries to ape a true care for the surfaces for which it is intended. Ornament is 'rhetoric' and Pound is implying a relationship between the 'rhetoric' of architecture and the 'rhetoric' of the other arts – either 'fussy' and degenerate or simple and dignified. This Imagist and Vorticist distinction conforms to Pound's general aesthetic, as do the constant references to London as a 'chaos', a disgorging spray in need of a 'vortex'. A curious image of Pound as the Baudelairean 'flâneur' walking the streets of London in search of 'an aesthetic of good city building' emerges. The quest seems to have begun at San Zeno in 1911 but above all Pound remembered later the years when, as 'B. H. Dias', 'I spent my odd time for several months observing the decadence of wood-carving, fan-lights over London doors.'[145] These words, written in 1937, come after Pound's economic 'enlightenment' when he was able to argue that 'the London ground rents and entail, lease system etc. have defiled English Building'.[146] In 1917 and 1918 Pound was still, relatively, an aesthete.

Observatory Gardens, Campden Hill, Kensington

It is said that architecture is the first of the arts to arrive in a civilisation. In the middle of the last century architecture gave way to plumbing and sanitation. The best minds in the building trade were not builders but plumbers. An inspection of London's Streets can lead to no other conclusion . . . the art of making house-fronts has been wholly eliminated by drains.[147]

Pound found employment for the suffragette's 'rusting hammers' in smashing cheap machine-made ornament and gave an A B C of 'How to look at a house front' in a uniform row of houses or a block. It was

(a) a matter of the composition of window parallelograms in the whole, (b) ornamentation. Take the most hideous houses in London: the row of six story plus basement red striped with yellow abominations of Observatory Avenue (sic), Campden Hill. No jerry-built horror of Clapham exceeds the rankness of these huge hideosities. . . . The height of the windows has been graduated, but not their breadth, *and* the windows are set too close together. The whole effect is appalling . . . The process by which one discovers this, *despite* the bewilderment of bad mouldings, stripes of hideous colour, convolutions, and so on, is the same as the process whereby one determines that any picture in any sort of art show is well or ill composed.[148]

The facade of the urban 'multiplied unit' was Pound's main concern, and in support of his argument he cited Palladio who began, he believed, 'by getting good facades and much Italian renaissance work got no further'.[149] For his own times Pound envisaged some intuitive calculus by which facades might be designed.

Pound also considered 'special buildings' – churches, hotels, large shops and so on. The Christian Science Church in Half Moon Street, off Piccadilly, he applauded because it was set into its lot with a commendable concern for its relationship to its surroundings and with an eye for its vistas.

The rarity of what would seem the simplest forms of common-sense in the arts is almost amazing. The curve of the girders or arches inside this church is excellent. The architect has shown a natural talent, or an acquired talent, or at any rate a fine feeling, for space.[150]

He is critical, however, of the set of the window frames and the 'defective' ornament.

Edward Wadsworth, design for a vorticist facade, 1919

In 1919 Pound reviewed Wadsworth's rather monstrous facade for a Vorticist building which caused a 'stir and hullabaloo', following 'perturbation' over Lewis's 'The Caliph's Design (Architects, where is your Vortex?)' (1919):

> Apart from our natural horror that any man should think of designing a building like Messrs. Lyons' Corner House, or the dwellings in Observatory Gardens . . . we remain calm enough to observe that Mr Wadsworth's model . . . is covered with curious ridges and excrescences.[151]

The problem of poor light in London particularly bothered Pound and he saw Wadsworth's facade as an attempt to attract what light there was. Pound also suggested that houses be terraced away from the street and that they should be intelligently oriented. 'How many dozens of corner houses have I not seen with blank walls to the west and windows facing north!'[152] Wadsworth's design also had the virtues of 'considering the properties of his material; the structural laws of ferroconcrete differ from those of stone construction'.[153] Pound, in an earlier article, had dealt with steel structures and the American acceptance of the metal's nature as distinct from a British attempt to treat it like stone or just disguise it.

Finally, and quite understandably, a view was given of the role of sculpture in the architectural environment. The Ritz, for instance, might have been 'almost interesting as a building' if a young sculptor had been allowed to adorn it who could have done his job 'as cheaply as the four-by-six stone cutter'. A promising event had been the Epstein statues in the Strand, but most sculpture for buildings was a disappointment. Pound found it 'incredible that with some of the best sculpture in the world stored in the British Museum English sculpture should have stuck dead in the Albert memorial period for so many years'. He deplored the need to complete the sculptural embellishment of buildings when there was obviously a dearth of talent:

> One could at least leave the blocks in the rough until the talent arrived . . . When one thinks of Gaudier-Brzeska too poor to buy stone for his work, one can readily believe that had the Ritz blocks been left rough, he would have been often only too glad to carve them at a guinea a mask; and Piccadilly would have been that much the richer.[154]

It was not until Pound had been in Paris for a few years that he fully began to develop and order these ideas on the centrality of architecture and its relationship to painting and sculpture. The fitful experimentation of Epstein's public sculpture, of the decorations at the Cave of the Golden Calf Cabaret, of Lewis's work at Lady Drogheda's house and at the Restaurant de la Tour Eiffel, and of the, mostly, 'unacceptable' Omega workshops had given Pound, as yet, no coherent vision of such a relationship.

The Ritz, Piccadilly, facade sculpture, 1906

XII

In the February–March 1919 issue of *The Little Review* Pound published his article the 'Death of Vorticism' which denied that such a fatality had occurred: Gaudier's influence was recently felt through his 1918 memorial exhibition; Wadsworth's camouflage for naval ships was an outstanding success and an example of government 'approval'; Vorticism *had* managed to educate the eye; and Lewis had been taken on as an official war artist. 'Obituary notices from New Zealand, Oregon, Bloomsbury and other suburbs will be read with interest by "i vorticisti" . . .'[155] But Pound knew the movement had, at least, gone into a prolonged temporary abeyance and that the 'moment' of 1914 had passed. In May 1920 Pound and Dorothy Shakespear went to Italy, and then, in June, to Paris. After a brief return to London the couple moved to Paris at the end of 1920. A new period in Ezra Pound's life was about to begin as he looked for a new 'vortex'.

Notes

1 'Et Faim Sallir le Coup des Boys', *Blast 2* (1915) (Santa Barbara, 1981), p.22.

2 *Selected Letters of Ezra Pound, 1907–1941*, ed. D. D. Paige (London, 1982), p.27.

3 See Noel Stock, *The Life of Ezra Pound* (Harmondsworth, 1985), *passim*, and *Letters*, *passim*.

4 Affirmations III: 'Jacob Epstein', *The New Age* (21 January 1915), pp.311–12 (*Ezra Pound and the Visual Arts*, ed. Harriet Zinnes (New York, 1980), p.10).

5 'To Whistler, American', *Poetry* (October 1912), p.7 (Zinnes, pp.217–18; *Collected Shorter Poems of Ezra Pound* (London, 1984), p.235).

6 Letter to Isabel W. Pound, 7 January 1909 (Zinnes, p.287).

7 'Whistler', *The New Age* (12 September 1912), p.466 (Zinnes, p.2).

8 *Letters*, p.44 (Zinnes, p.272). See also 'The Renaissance', *Poetry* (March, 1915) (*Literary Essays of Ezra Pound*, ed. T. S. Eliot, London, 1954, pp.214–26).

9 'On his own face in a glass', *Collected Shorter Poems of Ezra Pound* (London, 1984), p.35.

10 'Vortex. Pound', *Blast 1* (1914) (Santa Barbara, 1981), p.154.

11 *Gaudier-Brzeska: a Memoir* (New York, 1970), pp.119–20.

12 *Ibid.*, p.120.

13 *Ibid.*, p. 122.

14 See Stock, pp.67–143.

15 Hugh Kenner, *The Pound Era* (London, 1972), pp.323–6. See also p.137 of this catalogue.

16 *Imagist Poetry*, ed. Peter Jones (London, 1972), pp.124–34.

17 *Ibid.*, p.130.

18 *Ibid.*, p.131.

19 *Blast 2*, p.82.

20 Unpublished letter, Yale University Library.

21 *Collected Shorter Poems*, p.109.

22 'Vorticism', *Fortnightly Review* (1 September 1914), pp.46–71 (Zinnes, pp.199–209).

23 Affirmations VI: 'Analysis of this Decade', *The New Age* (11 February 1915), pp.409–11 (Zinnes, p.26).

24 For Hulme see Richard Cork, *Vorticism and Abstract Art in the First Machine Age*, 2 vols. (London, 1976), vol.1, pp.132–44, 185–213. See also William C. Wees, *Vorticism and the English Avant-Garde* (Toronto, 1972), pp.77–85, and Alan R. Jones, *The Life and Opinions of T. E. Hulme* (London, 1960).

25 Jacob Epstein, *Epstein: An Autobiography* (New York, 1955), p.60.

26 'This Hulme Business', *Townsman II*, (January 1939), p.15.

27 For a recent discussion of Bergson's influence on Hulme, Pound and others see Alan Robinson, *Poetry, Painting and Ideas, 1885–1914* (London, 1985), which also gives an indispensable background to Pound's activities in England during this period.

28 Wilhelm Worringer, *Abstraction and Empathy: A Contribution to the Psychology of Style*, trans. Michael Bullock (New York, 1955), p.42.

29 T. E. Hulme, *Speculations: Essays on Humanism and the Philosophy of Art*, ed. Herbert Read (London, 1924), p.78 (Cork, p.140).

30 *Ibid.*, p.82.

31 *Ibid.*, p.104.

32 *Ibid.*, pp.104–7.

33 *Ibid.*

34 *Ibid.*

35 'The Translator's Preface to Sorel's "Reflections on Violence"', *The New Age* (October 1915).

36 *The Cantos of Ezra Pound*, 3rd edn (London, 1975), p.71.

37 See George Dangerfield, *The Strange Death of Liberal England*, 2nd edn (London, 1970).

38 See Cork and Wees, *passim*.

39 Wees, chapter 4.

40 *Blast 1*, p.153.

41 *Ibid.*

42 In *A Lume Spento* (Venice, 1908), p.44.

43 William French and Timothy Materer, 'Far Flung Vortices and Ezra's "Hindoo" Yogi', *Paideuma*, 11, no.1 (1982), pp.39–49. See also Timothy Materer, *Vortex. Pound, Eliot and Lewis* (Ithaca, NY, 1979), which contains an excellent appraisal of Pound's interest in the visual arts.

44 French and Materer, p.44.

45 C. W. Leadbetter produced an interesting diagram of the Vortex in his book *The Chakras*, which is reproduced in French and Materer.

[46] *Blast 1*, p.153.
[47] *Ibid.*
[48] *Ibid.*, p.154.
[49] *Ibid.*
[50] 'Vorticism' (Zinnes, p.200).
[51] *Ibid.* (Zinnes, p.202).
[52] *Ibid.* (Zinnes, p.207).
[53] See *Blast 2*, p.34. In a letter to Wyndham Lewis (25 January 1949), Pound wrote that it was Gaudier's death that had prompted his 'serious curiosity' about politics and economics. See Materer, *Vortex*, p.63, and pp.63–106 for Pound and Gaudier.
[54] See Stock, p.182.
[55] *Ibid.*, p.185.
[56] *Ibid.*, p.78.
[57] *Blast 2*, p.86.
[58] *Ibid.*
[59] *Gaudier*, p.46.
[60] Affirmations v: 'Gaudier Brzeska', *The New Age* (4 February 1915), pp.409–11. (Zinnes, p.19).
[61] *Gaudier*, p.75.
[62] *Ibid.*, pp.146–7.
[63] See Stock, p.249.
[64] *ABC of Reading* (London, 1961) p.3.
[65] See Hugh Kenner, *The Pound Era* (London, 1972) for a discussion of Pound's interest in the ideogram. Also Earl Miner, *The Japanese Tradition in British and American Literature* (Princeton, NJ, 1958).
[66] *Gaudier*, p.76.
[67] *Ibid.*, p.50.
[68] See Cork, vol 1, pp.179–83.
[69] Allen Upward, *The New Word* (London, 1908).
[70] See Stock, p.179.
[71] *Gaudier*, p.49.
[72] A Prefatory Note to the Catalogue of A Memorial Exhibition of the Work of Henri Gaudier-Brzeska, Leicester Galleries, London, May–June 1918 (Zinnes, pp.249–52).
[73] *Ibid.* (Zinnes, p.251).
[74] *Gaudier*, p.130.
[75] *Shorter Poems*, p.74.
[76] *Gaudier*, p.39.
[77] *Ibid.*, p.39.
[78] *Ibid.*, p.40.
[79] *Ibid.*, p.48. See also p.121 of this catalogue.
[80] *Ibid.*, p.48.
[81] *Ibid.*, p.60n.
[82] Exhibition at the Goupil Gallery, *The Egoist* (16 March 1914), p.10 (Zinnes, p.183).
[83] 'The New Sculpture', *The Egoist* (16 February 1914), pp.67–8 (Zinnes, p.181).
[84] Affirmations III: 'Jacob Epstein', pp.311–12 (Zinnes, p.11).
[85] *Ibid.* (Zinnes, p.12).
[86] *Ibid.* (Zinnes, p.13).
[87] *Ibid.*
[88] Gaudier-Brzeska, 'The Allied Artists' Association Ltd., Holland Park Hall', *The Egoist* (15 June 1914) (Cork, vol.2, p.443). See also p.100 of this catalogue.
[89] 'Exhibition at the Goupil Gallery', p.109 (Zinnes, p.183).
[90] 'The New Sculpture', pp.67–8 (Zinnes, p.181).
[91] 'Exhibition at the Goupil Gallery' (see note 89) (Zinnes, p.10).
[92] Art Notes: 'The Loan Exhibition at the Grafton', *The New Age* (20 December 1917), pp.152–3 (Zinnes, pp.34–6).
[93] *Letters*, p.74 (Zinnes, p.279).
[94] Art Notes: *The New Age* (11 December 1919), pp.96–7 (Zinnes, p.126).
[95] *Ibid.* (Zinnes, p.127).
[96] 'Wyndham Lewis', *The Egoist* (15 June 1914), pp.233–4 (Zinnes, p.187).
[97] *Ibid.* (Zinnes, p.188).
[98] *Ibid.*
[99] *Ibid.*
[100] *Letters*, p.74.
[101] 'Wyndham Lewis', pp.233–4 (Zinnes, p.189).
[102] Letter to Quinn, 18 April 1915 (Zinnes, p.230).
[103] Letter to Quinn, 13 July 1916 (Zinnes, p.238).
[104] *Ibid.*
[105] *Ibid.*
[106] *Ibid.*
[107] Affirmations II: 'Vorticism', pp.277–8 (Zinnes, p.7).
[108] *Ibid.* (Zinnes, pp.7–8).
[109] *Blast 2*, p.19; see also Zinnes, p.153 n.4.
[110] *Blast 1*, p.49.
[111] 'Edward Wadsworth. Vorticist', *The Egoist* (15 August 1914), pp.306–7 (Zinnes, pp.190–3).
[112] Art Notes: *The New Age* (27 March 1919), p.342 (Zinnes, p.108).
[113] *Ibid.*
[114] 'Edward Wadsworth. Vorticist', pp.306–7 (Zinnes, pp.192–3).
[115] Letter to Harriet Monroe, 1914 (Zinnes, pp.288–9).
[116] *Ibid.*
[117] Affirmations II: 'Vorticism' (Zinnes, p.9).
[118] *Ibid.*
[119] 'Inner Necessity', *Blast 1*, pp.119–25.

Kandinsky's book was first published in a full English translation, by M. T. H. Sadleir, in 1914.

[120] 'Edward Wadsworth. Vorticist', pp.306–7 (Zinnes, p.193).

[121] 'Arnold Dolmetsch', *The New Age* (7 January 1915), pp.246–7.

[122] *Gaudier*, p.127.

[123] Quoted in Jacob Korg, 'Jacob Epstein's Rock Drill and the Cantos', *Paideuma*, 4, nos.2 and 3 (1975), pp.301–13.

[124] Letter to Quinn, 18 March 1916 (in B. L. Reid, *The Man from New York. John Quinn and his Friends* (New York, 1968), p.248).

[125] See Archie Henderson, 'Pound's *Strelets* Interview (1915)', in *Paideuma*, 11, no.3 (1982), pp.473–87.

[126] Affirmations VI: 'Analysis of this Decade', pp.409–11 (Zinnes, p.24).

[127] *Ibid.* (Zinnes, pp.25–6).

[128] *Ibid.* (Zinnes, pp.26–9).

[129] Reid, p.3. See also Judith Zilcher, 'The Noble Buyer: John Quinn, Patron of the Avant-Garde', Catalogue for an exhibition at the Hirshhorn Museum, 1978, and p.136 of this catalogue.

[130] Letter to Pound, 25 February 1915 (Reid, p.198).

[131] Letter to Quinn, 8 March 1915 (Reid, p.199).

[132] *Ibid.*

[133] *Ibid.*, p.253.

[134] See Stock, p.177.

[135] *Alvin Langdon Coburn, Photographer: An Autobiography*, ed. Helmut and Alison Gernsheim (London, 1966), p.102.

[136] Catalogue introduction for exhibition 'Vortographs and Paintings by A. L. Coburn' (Zinnes, pp.154–7).

[137] *Ibid.*

[138] Art Notes: *The New Age* (6 June 1918), p.91 (Zinnes, p.59). For an account of the *New Age* 'circle' and its influential author, A. R. Orage, see Wallace Martin, *The New Age under Orage*: Chapters in *English Cultural History* (Manchester, 1967).

[139] Art Notes: *The New Age* (18 July 1918), p.189 (Zinnes, pp.67–8).

[140] 'Wyndham Lewis at the Goupil', *The New Age* (20 February 1919) (Zinnes, p.100).

[141] See Zinnes, pp.30–145, for Pound's 'Art Notes'.

[142] Art Notes: 'Buildings – 1', *The New Age* (29 August 1918), pp.287–8 (Zinnes, pp.75–6).

[143] Art Notes: 'Buildings: Ornamentation!', *The New Age* (12 September 1918), p.320 (Zinnes, p.76).

[144] Art Notes: 'Buildings – 1', pp.287–8 (Zinnes, p.74).

[145] *Guide to Kulchur* (New York, 1968), p.245.

[146] *Ibid.*

[147] Art Notes: 'Parallelograms', *The New Age* (17 October 1918), pp.400–1 (Zinnes, p.81).

[148] *Ibid.* (Zinnes, pp.82–3).

[149] Art Notes: 'Super Fronts', *The New Age* (24 October 1918), p.414 (Zinnes, p.84).

[150] *Ibid.*

[151] Art Notes: *The New Age* (11 December 1919), pp.96–7 (Zinnes, pp.126–7).

[152] *Ibid.*

[153] *Ibid.*

[154] Art Notes: 'Super Fronts', p.414 (Zinnes, p.85).

[155] 'The Death of Vorticism', *The Little Review* (February/March 1919), pp.45 and 48 (Zinnes, pp.209–10).

Parenthetical Paris, 1920–1925
Pound, Picabia, Brancusi and Léger

JOHN ALEXANDER

I

Some fifteen years after the event, Ezra Pound looked back at the aftermath of Imagism in London and recalled how (in 1917 or 1918), seeking a new formality for their poetry, he and T. S. Eliot had turned to the example of Théophile Gautier.

> That is to say, at a particular date in a particular room, two authors, neither engaged in picking the other's pocket, decided that the dilutation of *vers libre*, Amygism, Lee Masterism, general floppiness had gone too far and that some counter-current must be set going. Parallel situation centuries ago in China. Remedy prescribed 'Emaux et Camées' (or the Bay State Hymn Book). Rhyme and regular strophes. Results: Poems in Mr Eliot's second volume . . . also 'H. S. Mauberley'.[1]

Gautier's poem 'L'Art' in *Emaux et Camées* figures the process of creating a work of art in terms of a sculptor's struggle with a recalcitrant medium, and recommends that struggle:

> Oui, l'oeuvre sort plus belle
> D'une forme au travail
> Rebelle,
> Vers, marbre, onyx, émail.
> . . .
>
> Statuaire, repousse
> L'argile que pétrit
> Le pouce
> Quand flotte ailleurs l'esprit;
>
> Lutte avec le carrare,
> Avec le paros dur
> Et rare,

Gardiens du contour pur;

. . .

Les dieux eux-mêmes meurent
Mais les vers souverains
    Demeurent
Plus forts que les airains.

Sculpte, lime, cisèle;
Que ton rêve flottant
    Se scelle
Dans le bloc résistant![2]

It was 'hardness' which Pound singled out as the achievement of Gautier, the sense that out of struggle had been brought something of enduring beauty, like a piece of sculpture.[3]

If Pound seems to have known and been influenced by Gautier's work earlier than the writing of *Hugh Selwyn Mauberley*,[4] it is difficult not to suppose that his understanding of it was deepened by his friendship in London with the sculptor Henri Gaudier-Brzeska, who 'cut direct', and whose programmatic 'Vortex' alone Pound predicted would 'become the text-book in all academies of sculpture before our generation has passed from the earth'.[5]

Such enduring achievement of the beautiful, γοκαλότ, is debased, 'Decreed in the market place', in *Hugh Selwyn Mauberley*.[6] Again, the bitterness of these lines may also derive from Pound's knowledge of the treatment meted out to Gaudier-Brzeska.

The first piece of sculpture that he was commissioned to make was the statue of Maria Carmi. I am told he was promised £100 for this work, from people well able to pay it. 'They ended by giving him £5.'[7]

Pound seems to satirise in *Hugh Selwyn Mauberley* the preference of the age for the 'pianola', for 'tawdry cheapness', over pure and lasting beauty.

The age demanded an image
Of its accelerated grimace,
Something for the modern stage,
Not, at any rate, an Attic grace;

Not, not certainly, the obscure reveries
Of the inward gaze;
Better mendacities
Than the classics in paraphrase!

[82]

> The 'age demanded' chiefly a mould in plaster,
> Made with no loss of time,
> A prose kinema, not, not assuredly, alabaster
> Or the 'sculpture' of rhyme.[8]

However close Pound's own art, 'his tool/The engraver's',[9] is to that of Mauberley, he is still in two minds about 'the "sculpture" of rhyme', and puts it in inverted commas because he wants to distance himself from it. In his essay 'The hard and soft in French poetry', Pound distinguishes in Gautier a 'hardness' which is intent upon conveying a particular quality of emotion – as Gaudier-Brzeska had said that his head of Pound would convey 'certain emotions'[10] – from the 'frigid' art of Hérédia, whose hardness was no more than the attempt to be poetic.[11]

The importance of the accurate expression of feeling over the mere poetic also comes across in Pound's lines on the poet's perception.

> He made no immediate application
> Of this to relation of the state
> To the individual, the month was more temperate
> Because this beauty had been.[12]

For what Pound cannot tolerate, despite and perhaps because of a tendency towards this himself which produces the ambiguities of Mauberley, is the art that is estranged from the world, as mere 'rhetoric', art for art's sake.[13] In this sense too he had execrated 'the school of sentimental aesthetics' which could not perceive beauty in the forms of the modern world: 'This enjoyment of machinery is just as natural and just as significant a phase of this age as was the Renaissance "enjoyment of nature for its own sake".'[14]

If we forget the mechanistic vocabulary of Vorticism, assuming too readily that phrases like 'prose kinema' and 'accelerated grimace' are categorically disparaging, we are in danger of misreading some aspects of Pound's 'parenthetical Paris'.[15] Instead I would like to suggest that an understanding of these years, in between the Vortex of London and the ideal landscape of *The Cantos*, Italy, may be approached through an intuition of two poles in Pound's thought. They are poles which in some sense correspond to the vortex and to the ideal landscape, and which are manifest in *Hugh Selwyn Mauberley*: on the one hand we find the satirical and dynamic polemic clearing away the moribund and the rhetorical, and on the other the pursuit of a pure and formal beauty.

In the spring of 1920 Ezra Pound left London with his wife for a holiday in Italy.[16] They stayed in Venice and Sirmione, and returning in June broke their journey in Paris, where they helped James Joyce to settle in. That month Pound's *Hugh Selwyn Mauberley* was published in London.[17]

Later in the year Pound wrote from London a series of 'Island of Paris' articles for the American journal *The Dial*. In the first of these he tells how he had gone to Paris that June 'seeking the triple extract of literature for export purposes; seeking a poetic serum to save English letters from postmature and American telegraphics from premature suicide and decomposition'.[18]

'Which brings us', in Pound's own words in *The Dial*, 'to the young and very ferocious . . .':

> The young began in Zurich about two years ago, they have published papers which are very, very erratic in appearance, and which contain various grains of good sense.
>
> They have satirized the holy church of our century (journalism), they have satirized the sanctimonious attitude toward 'the arts' (toward the arts irrespective of whether the given work of art contains a communication of intelligence). They have given up the pretense of impartiality. They have expressed a desire to live and to die, preferring death to a sort of moribund permanence.
>
> They are so young and healthy that they still consider suicide as a possible remedy for certain troubles . . .[19]
>
> They have as yet no capital sunk in works and they indulge in the pious hope that their remains will not be used to bore others . . .
>
> Louis Aragon, Phillippe Soupault, André Breton, Drieu la Rochelle contribute to Littérature and are published Au Sans Pareil. They are, I think officially, on good terms with Tristan Tzara, Picasso, Piccabia [sic].
>
> One wonders, a little vaguely, how to introduce them to a society where one is considered decadent for reproducing pictures by Cézanne.[20]

What had occurred in Zurich 'about two years' before this was written was the reading in July 1918 of Tristan Tzara's second Dada manifesto, subsequently published in *Dada 3* the following December, incorporating for the first time in this magazine Francis Picabia's 'erratic' typography.[21] Picabia (1879–1953) had been in New York and Tristan Tzara in Zurich where Dada had had its simultaneous beginnings in 1915–16. It was, however, in Zurich that the word 'Dada' had first been used,[22] and it was there that Picabia and Tzara met in February 1919.[23] In the spring of that year Picabia moved to Paris and was joined by Tzara on 5 January 1920.[24] Tzara's manifesto had meanwhile been the 'principal channel' through which Dada ideas reached Louis Aragon, Phillippe Soupault, André Breton and others in Paris.[25] When Picabia and Tzara arrived Breton had already begun publishing his magazine *Littérature* with the assistance of Soupault and Aragon.[26]

Six months before the letter in *The Dial* Pound had himself been responsible for a note on the removal of Zurich Dada to Paris contributed to one of the group's 'erratic' papers, Tzara's *Dadaphone* (*Dada 7*) of March 1920.

> DADA No 1. Quelques jeunes hommes intelligents stranded in Zurich desire correspondence with other unfortunates similarly situated in other godforsaken corners of the earth.
> DADA: Bulletin 5 feb. Ils ont échappé. They have got to Paris. La bombe!! Là ZUT-excelsior!!
> London.   EZRA POUND.

The note suggests that Pound was already looking beyond England for another group of which he could be a part. It suggests that he felt a sympathy for these 'unfortunates', these 'intelligent' young men, stuck like him in a 'godforsaken corner'. On Pound's part there seems to be an anticipation of the sense of release to be felt on arriving in Paris. For though Paris was in some ways as bad as London, if not worse,[27] the assault on 'sanctimoniousness' which Dada represented for Pound, and its lack of 'impartiality', were both characteristics of his own writings about art from the earliest days – with his talk of 'a race with brains like rabbits' and his contribution 'To the present condition of things we have nothing to say but "merde"'[28] – and which were well represented in *Blast*.

In the same month as the *Dial* letter quoted above, Pound also appeared in French as Dada's English correspondent, 'votre bien dévoué', in Breton's *Littérature*: 'Vous me demandez de vous écrire les noms de ceux qui à mon avis ont essayé de détruire la bêtise dans le brumeux séjour britannique.'[29] Though Pound clearly felt the need to be part of a group – he felt that the 'good talk and wide interest' of the Renaissance court were now to be found in artists' studios, and that the important distinction was no longer between '"bohème" and "bourgeois"' but among artists themselves – the list he gives shows how different his own conception of the individual artist still was from that of the Dadaists.[30] He cites Thomas Hardy, W. H. Hudson, Henry James ('il avait aussi beaucoup embêté M. Gustave Flaubert, de sainte et vénérable mémoire'), W. B. Yeats, Ford Madox Hueffer ('qui a lutté contre la littérature officielle seul pendant vingt ans, notre meilleur critique, auquel on doit offrir chaque année le sang et les os de cent mille gosses'), James Joyce ('qui écrit de la prose pour tuer'), Wyndham Lewis, Henri Gaudier-Brzeska, and T. S. Eliot ('le malin . . . qui a lu Laforgue plus soigneusement que les compatriotes du dit Jules, et qui y a ajouté quelque chose'). For Pound the study of literature is 'hero-worship',[31] and the artist is distinguished by the impress of his intelligence in his work – for which we have seen Gautier as the paradigm. It was because he thought their poetry set less value upon the individual that Pound retained his 'full suspicion of agglomerates' when reading the Unanimists.[32]

Despite Dada's dismantling of established art and its attitudes it was to the satiric tradition of Laforgue (who 'marks the next phase in French poetry after Gautier'[33]) that Pound in *The Dial* managed to assimilate both them and Eliot:

> Carrying on the satiric heritage of Laforgue, and of symboliste sonorities this group is already taking its place in the sun, by right of intelligence, more than by right of work yet accomplished.[34]

Pound had never been able quite to square the Unanimist group with this tradition from Gautier to Laforgue, even if at one time they had been 'the only one which seems to me to have an energy comparable to that of the *Blast* group in London, and is the only group in which the writers for *Blast* can be expected to take very much interest'.[35] But if the stultification of London played its part in his decision to leave – 'England has always loved the man incapable of thought'[36] – it was perhaps what he identified as the 'intelligence' of the 'intelligent' young men of Zurich and Paris that was finally most important in his choice of the latter city. It was the 'acumen' of Julien Benda,[37] and, as we shall see, the 'thought' of Picabia, that he valued, and numerous references show the same to be true of Jean Cocteau, who formed 'the most long-lived of Pound's ties to the French avant-garde'.[38] It was certainly their satire of the sanctimony of belief and the 'partiality' of their discrimination that most contrasted with the thought-cramping atmosphere of London.[39]

By Christmas 1920 Pound and his wife had moved into a flat at 70 bis, rue Notre-Dame des Champs.[40] That month Francis Picabia exhibited at the Galerie Povolozky.[41] The Pounds spent the first three months of 1921 at Saint-Raphaël on the Côte d'Azur.[42] Here 'Christian' (Georges Herbiet, 1895–1969), a writer, painter –

> What the deuce has Herbiet (Christian)
> done with his painting?   (Canto LXXX)[43]

– and critic, had opened an imaginatively stocked bookshop, Au Bel Exemplaire, in October of 1920, which was patronised by Pound, Picabia, Crotti, Gleizes, Raoul Dufy and others.[44] Poupard-Lieussou tells us that 'Christian' had met Picabia (through Crotti) and Pound in the spring of 1919, the latter at the Galerie Povolozky,[45] and had become one of Picabia's closest friends. In Saint-Raphaël Pound sought out 'Christian' for conversation and tennis,[46] and whatever the qualities of Au Bel Exemplaire, wrote to Ford Madox Ford that he had not yet seen *Jésus-Christ Rastaquouère*, by the 'skittish Piccabia' [sic].[47]

Pound returned to Paris in April. On the 12th of that month he asked Francis Picabia to become the Foreign Editor of *The Little Review*, of which he was himself now the European Editor, resuming an earlier connection which had all but lapsed by 1921.[48]

PAINTINGS
"CHRISTIAN"

The Little Review, Spring 1922

During his London years, from 1914 onwards, Pound had scorned Picabia's art in his reviews and his letters to the American patron and collector John Quinn, as 'froth', 'pretty brightness', and as imitative of the work of artists with whom Pound was himself at the time associated.[49] Although these terms come close to the epithet 'skittish', it seems likely that this, and the misspelling of Picabia's name in the letter to Ford as in the 'Island of Paris', indicate that what had begun to change Pound's mind about Picabia was the latter's personality at least as much as his writing. In April Pound wrote to Agnes Bedford, who was later to help him with his opera *Le Testament de Villon*, 'find Cocteau and Picabia intelligent',[50] and it is as a thinker and a 'live animal' that he describes Picabia to John Quinn.[51]

William Carlos Williams criticised Pound's taste in this great period of Picasso, Juan Gris, Braque and Matisse – 'who among all these people do you think Pound picked as his champion? Picabia, a purely literary figure, Picabia and Léger'.[52] Although it was as a writer that Pound wanted to include Picabia, along with Wyndham Lewis, Picasso and Brancusi, in a book on *Four Modern Artists* that never came to fruition,[53] his early reserve about the paintings[54] is moderated

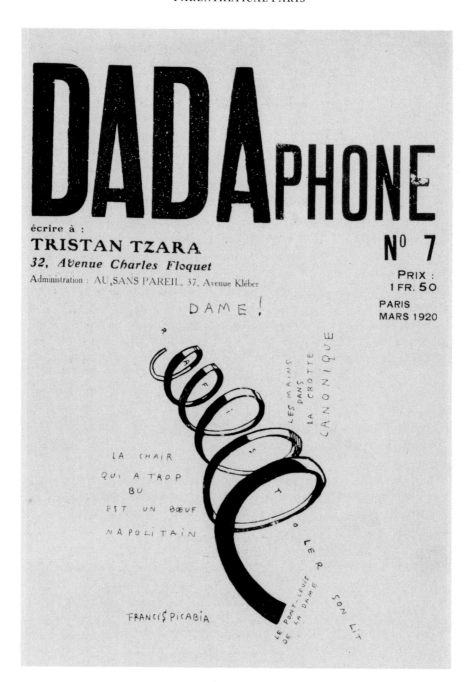

Dadaphone, *Dada*, no. 7, March 1920, cover

when he ventures that 'there is more in his design stuff than comes up in reproduction'.[55] This may well refer to Picabia's more recent work on Dada periodicals, as for instance his cover for Tzara's *Dadaphone*, to which Pound had contributed.

Older than Breton, Soupault and Aragon, Picabia had first painted as an Impressionist, and had then moved through Orphic Cubism (and friendship with Apollinaire)[56] with Marcel Duchamp – his associate from the Piteaux group – toward increasingly machine-like forms.[57] In New York, where he had been part of the circle around Alfred Stieglitz (which included William Carlos Williams, Mina Loy, Marcel Duchamp and Man Ray), and the Dada magazine *291*, Picabia had arrived at a simplified draughtsmanship accompanied by an 'erratic', almost childlike script, for the presentation of real or imagined pieces of machinery. It is this tendency in his art[58] which is exemplified in the cover of *Dadaphone* and in the work that he did on his own magazine *391* (published on his travels between 1917 and 1924 variously in Barcelona, New York, Lausanne, Zurich and Paris). The satirical and iconoclastic nature of the machine pictures, at once suggesting the mechanisation of man – or, more often, woman – and de-sanitising and de-idealising the machine by bringing it within the realm of the erotic, is also apparent in two works reproduced in the March 1920 issue of *391*: Picabia's version of Marcel Duchamp's punning 'LHOOQ',[59] and his own ink blot, 'La Sainte Vierge'.

LA SAINTE-VIERGE

FRANCIS PICABIA

391, no.12, March 1920

[89]

Writing on the literature of Paris in the *Literary Review* of the New York *Evening Post*,[60] Pound now declared that, although he 'is not a bad painter', 'I do not present him as a painter':

Take away the painting and there would still be nearly all of Picabia: Picabia, the man who, in ten lines and an almost photographic drawing of a wheel or a valve will dissociate, or satirize, or at any rate expose 'all the formal thought or invention' that a salon painter or secondary cubist employs in a 'picture'.

He is not a 'master', as are Brancusi, Picasso and Matisse, but he does work

in a definite medium, to which one may give an interim label of thought. In his beautiful and clear pictures, which cannot be reproduced by half-tone blocks, there is perhaps no sign of visual sensitivity, or at least of that kind of visual *receptivity* which underlies the nervous outlines of a Picasso, but there is a very clear exteriorization of Picabia's mental activity.

Whereas Picasso, Pound suggests, 'never had an idea in his life', Picabia he values for his 'mental activity'. As a writer, in *Pensées sans langage* and *Jésus-Christ Rastaquouère*, Picabia acts as 'a sort of Socratic or anti-Socratic vacuum cleaner' upon the kinds of dogmatism and mental habit which Pound had found so intolerable in England. 'Picabia's philosophy moves stark naked' on a 'glassy surface', 'he can breathe and exist amid the unfurnished attitudes of negation, where British leader writers and members of the French literary chapels turn giddy or bleed at the mouth.'

Pound would not accept as literature Picabia's negation of propriety in 'the photograph of a letter of Ingres', but he added that 'an accumulation of such wild shots ends by expressing a personality'.[61] He attributed Picabia's 'nettoyage' – his cleaning up or cleaning out which effaced 'all colour, all representation, nearly all design' – to his 'love for the absolute'.[62]

An interesting light may be thrown upon this judgement, and upon the significance Dada possessed for Pound, by his publication in the magazine *Mécano*.[63] The editor, C. E. M. Küpper (1883–1931), is better known by his pseudonym of Theo van Doesburg, the name he used for his work in the plastic arts and his writing until about 1918.[64] But besides the formal and analytical work with De Stijl, for which he is best known, there is a complementary strand of Dada activity in his oeuvre, undertaken in the pages of his magazine *Mécano* and under the further pseudonym of I. K. Bonset.[65] Although the geometrical abstraction of Neo-plasticism and Elementarism seems utterly opposed to the anarchism of Dada, Van Doesburg believed in the continuous evolution of the spirit[66] that,

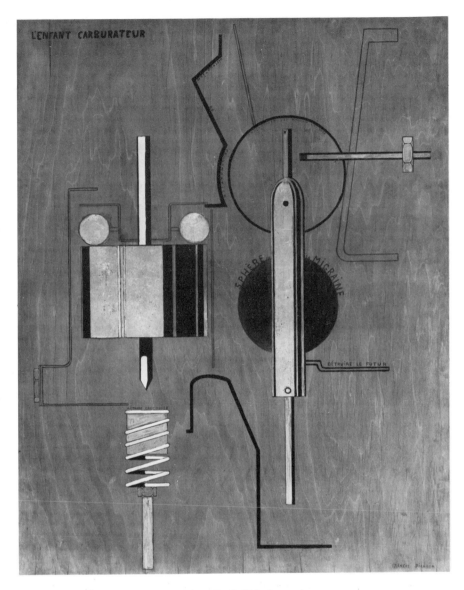

Francis Picabia, 'The Child Carburetor', 1919
Solomon R. Guggenheim Museum, New York

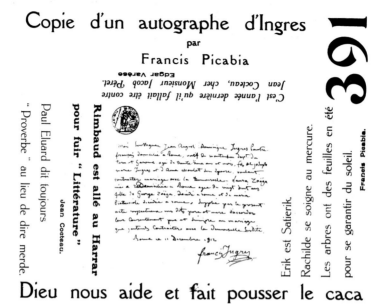

391, no.14, November 1920, detail of cover
copy of an Ingres letter by Francis Picabia

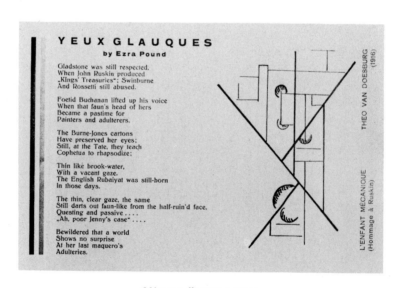

Mécano, yellow no.1, 1922

Only a radical cleansing of social and artistic life as, in the domain of art, is already done by Dada, which is anti-sentimental and healthy to the core since it is anti-art, only unscrupulously striking down any systematically bred amateurism in any field, can prepare civilization for the New Vision's happiness . . .[67]

Van Doesburg published Pound's 'Yeux Glauques' in the first issue of *Mécano*.[68] The poem at one and the same time celebrates and satirises the pre-Raphaelites. It also anticipates the way in which the divine is experienced through the physical in *The Cantos*:

> no vestige save in the air
> in stone is no imprint and the grey walls of no era
> under the olives
> saeculorum Athenae
> γλαύε γλαυκῶπιs
> olivi
> that which gleams and then does not gleam
> as the leaf turns in the air
>
> (Canto LXXIV)[69]

In the 'glassy surface' upon which Picabia's thought moved and in his 'beautiful and clear' pictures, Pound found something of those qualities of hardness and cleanness he had come to associate with the sculptural, here bent upon the act of cleansing.[70]

The month after Pound's return to Paris from Saint-Raphaël Picabia published in *Comoedia* his formal dissociation from Dada.[71] It seems that Picabia was increasingly dissatisfied with the movement's growing dogmatism under the influence of André Breton.[72] Two days later the 'trial' of the senior French writer and nationalist Maurice Barrès (1862–1923) was held, which Breton planned 'in all seriousness'[73] and over which he presided, with Ribemont-Dessaignes prosecuting, Aragon and Soupault acting for the defence, and Tzara amongst the witnesses.[74] It appears that Pound was present,[75] but Picabia left in the middle of the proceedings. 'Now Dada has a court, lawyers, soon probably police', he wrote in another article of renunciation published in *L'Esprit nouveau*.[76]

Picabia celebrated his freedom from Dada with a special issue of 391 entitled *Le Pilhaou-Thibaou* (10 July 1921), containing three contributions by Ezra Pound.[77] These are 'Christian's' translations (the first into French) of 'Moeurs Contemporaines' – some of which appeared again later in the year in the special Dada number (16 November 1921) of the Belgian magazine *Ça Ira*[78] – a remark taken from a letter to Picabia,[79] and printed along the margin of a page, 'Why Paris?

KONGO ROUX

Femme, moyen nécessaire pour la reproduction.
Disciple, moyen (pas nécessaire) pour la reproduction.
Reproduction, pas nécessaire.

Réformateur

Dit le cochon : « O que le monde soit porcin.

Souscrivez(naturellement)à l'emprunt Papal !   **SOUVENIR**
Pour la patrie, tant que vous voulez, Mais pour   Dernier auto-da-fé,
une Société anonyme de Pétrole, Mourir... Pourquoi ? Espagne a. d. 1759
                  Mourir. Inquisition rétablie
                                Portugal a.d. 1824
Historique
                            Souscrivez à l'

A Vérone on voit, voit encore, un orifice de boîte, E
c'est au Piazza dei Signori, un petit trou dans une M
tablette de marbre, avec l'inscription : Cette boîte est P
pour les dénonciations des usuriers et des contrats R
injustes d'usure. 1320-1921, on appelle ça le PROGRÈS. U
                                 N
Crédit
                                 T
Croyance que l'autre va payer. P
Crédit solide, croyance raisonnable que l'autre va payer. A
    Ça... dépend de la conduite de tous ; P
    Tous doivent avoir suffrage en tout ce qui concerne A
l'allocation des crédits... Ah ben oui. L
     C'est à vous, un tel, à 6 o/o
     C'est à vous, Fulano, à 30 o/o. Fiche-moi la paix.
Paixtrole.
     Fiche-moi la Paixtrole.
On veut les marchés de la lune. (O Jules unanime et Laforgue.)
Tout de même c'est l'Allemagne qui doit commencer,
        vu
vu que la France est fichue le jour où elle retire ses troupes des bords du Rhin.
     (ben oiu iou oui mong vieux, j'arrive de loing, pas d'illusion.)
vu que la France sera foutue, et que le Rhin était internationalisé par le traité d'il y a cent ans. C'est l'Allemagne qui doit commencer
en nous donnant un tout petit coin, un tout petit Heidelberg, ou un tout petit Schaffaausen pour ville DÉNATIONALISTE, ville
dénationaliste sans troupes, sans armée, sans aucune importance militaire, sans aucun gouvernement sauf pour balayer les rues,
et pomper le gaz et l'électricité (pouvoir de la houille blanche, le Rhin coule toujours).

On appellera
ça KONGO,
ou Venusberg
ou la nouvelle
Athènes selon

Les révolutions ont été beaucoup moins couteuses qu'on ne le suppose. Lisez Goncourt (qui n'aimait pas Mme Récamier) il dénonce le
mauvais goût du Directoire (ayant supporté plusieurs sortes de mauvais goût dans son temps) — et quand il veut dénigrer les sans-
culottes il trouve : LA NOTE, addition : plusieurs églises, plusieurs villas (très chics) et le mobilier — non détruit en masse, mais
plutôt vendu aux enchères, mis en vente sur les quais.
    JE NE VEUX PAS, non, je ne veux pas de révolution, *seulement* vu que nous sommes gouvernés par la finance, vu que la cause
des guerres est connue « aussi bien et clairement que la cause de la syphilis », c'est-à-dire la compétition pour vendre des « surplus »
dans un marché qui rétrécit...
    e voudrais, oui, je préférerais que les financiers gouvernassent directement qu'ils fussent responsables vis-à-vis des peuples ;
au lieu de gouverner par une quantité de sales types, choisis par eux (les financiers) responsables vis-à-vis des financiers et « élus »
par le peuple.
    Christianisme. malgré qu'il ne soit plus la croyance de l'homme pensant européen, il n'y a pas une seule coutume, loi, convention ni
de l'Europe, ni de l'Amérique qui ne soit pourrie à cause de cette base — totem de tribu SHEENY, Yid, taboo, pourriture
— Moïse habile politique — pourriture *monotheos.*
    MONOtheism, l'idée la plus crûment et immaturément idéologue, intellectuelle, maladivement cérébraliste, idée la moins fondée, la
moins prouvée qui ait jamais été avalée par 3/8 de la race humaine.
                          « 'Jésus-Christ était nègre. » (Voir les écrits
                                 de Marcus Garvey,
                                 un noir.)

                                 Ainsi San Zeno.
                                 Bravo Marcus !

SOMMAIRE

Femelle, chaos.
Mâle, point fixe de stupidité.
Femme, boulotte roulante sur quatre totems.... taboo et beretta.
Homme, particule imbécile magnétisée par l'inconnu.

$$\frac{\text{Le contrôle des crédits internationaux}}{\text{masque à gaz muselière}} = \frac{X}{\text{jeune homme}}$$

Etats-Unis d'Amérique, Diabetics'Union for the suppression of sugar.
    (Union des diabétiques pour la suppression du sucre)

                                          Ezra POUND.

Left margin (vertical): Ce sont les singes qui font les lieux-communs.

Far left margin (vertical): F. P.

Right margin (vertical): Il y a deux infinis : Dieu et la bêtise

Far right margin (vertical): Edgard VARÈSE.

Le Pilhaou-Thibaou, July 1921
Reprinted by permission of the Ezra Pound Literary Property Trust
and Faber and Faber Ltd. Copyright Ezra Pound 1921

Paris the centre of the world: Why? And I am here for three months without finding a congenial mistress', and a poem in French entitled 'Kongo Roux'. Whether the poem is by Pound, or was assembled by Picabia out of excerpts from his letters, the two men seem to have been planning it together at least as early as May of that year.[80]

In *Ça Ira* 'Christian's' translations of 'Moeurs Contemporaines' are indeed, in Serge Fauchereau's words, 'des poèmes fort peu dada'. With this in mind, Sanouillet's identification of 'Kongo Roux' as probably the first French Dada text with political implications seems to beg the question whether it is Dada at all.[81] What is more, Paris Dada seems to have been remarkable for its lack of political concern – an attitude perhaps exemplified by the reaction of Picabia to the Barrès affair, when the surrogate politics of artistic broadsides and polemic began to touch on real politics. Like Pound, Edmund Wilson saw Dada in direct descent from Symbolism, and explained the growing political commitment amongst Paris Dadaists like André Breton as a reaction against Dada's

> extreme stage of relativism . . . making a duty of irresponsibility and a morality of moral anarchism . . . they found that their necessary next progression took them out of the doctrine of relativity, which they had carried as far as was possible, and into beginning again with a creed and a code, fixed principles, a plan of action.[82]

The years between the wars have been described by one historian as 'an age of disinheritance . . . with a longing for a "breakthrough" toward simple resolutions and "authentic" goals'.[83] However tricky such diagnoses of the spirit of the age must always be, there is no doubt that Pound was impatient of what Spengler called the 'witty game',[84] nor that his review of Mina Loy and Marianne Moore seems to show a sympathy for the former's poetry written amidst the New York Dada circle. Logopoiea is, he says,

> in their case, the utterance of clever people in despair, or hovering upon the brink of that precipice. It is of those who have acceded with Renan 'La bêtise humaine est la seule chose qui donne une idée de l'infini'. It is a mind cry, more than a heart cry. 'Take the world if thou wilt but leave me an asylum for my affection' is not their lamentation, but rather 'In the midst of this desolation, give me at least one intelligence to converse with.'[85]

Though the apparently random ordering of the page-long 'Kongo Roux' has a Dada feel, as do the claim that Christ 'était nègre' and the references to sexual reproduction, those to Veronese history and San Zeno, to credit, usury and papal loans, recall *The Cantos* and the economic theories – so much founded upon the position of the artist ('give me at least one intelligence to converse with') and the quality of his art – which were to lead Pound into a fatal misreading of Mussolini after his move to Italy. In this connection it should also be noted that besides the issue of economics, Mussolini's self-projection as sculptor of the people so accorded with Pound's own terminology that he reiterated the idea himself.[86]

In the earliest letters from Paris Pound told of his plans for the special issues of *The Little Review* which he had in mind. The 'Brancusi Number' was published, with Pound and Picabia now appearing as editors, in the autumn of 1921. The issue contains, as well as Pound's essay on Brancusi to which we shall presently come, poems by Pound under the pseudonym of 'Abel Sanders'.[87] The poems are dedicated to William Carlos Williams and Baroness Elsa von Freytag-Loringhoven. The latter, an eccentric member of the New York Dada circle, had written a Dada review of Williams's experiment in automatic writing, *Kora in Hell*, which occasioned this reply by Pound.[88]

'Abel Sanders' also had a number of squibs in the 'Picabia Number' of *The Little Review* in the spring of 1922, which was partly funded by Picabia himself.[89] The issue contains reproductions of Picabia's work, which Pound had helped to choose,[90] three paintings by 'Christian', and a new calendar proposed by Pound and starting on his birthday – the day James Joyce finished *Ulysses*. This may suggest Pound's continuing interest in the occult; it recalls his proclamation of the 'END OF THE CHRISTIAN ERA' in advertisements for *Blast*, as well as looking forward to his use of the Fascist calendar of Mussolini.[91]

THE POEMS OF ABEL SANDERS

To Bill Williams and Else von Johann Wolfgang Loringhoven y Fulano

CODSWAY   bugwash
Bill's way   backwash
FreytagElse ¾arf an'arf
Billy Sunday one harf Kaiser Bill one harf
    Elseharf Suntag, Billsharf Freitag
Brot wit thranen,   con plaisir ou con patate   pomodoro

Bill dago resisting U.SAgo, Else ditto on the verb
basis yunker, plus Kaiser Bill reading to goddarnd stupid wife anbrats works
    of simple
domestic piety in Bleibtreu coner of Hockhoff'sbesitzendeecke
before the bottom fell out. Plus a little boiled Neitzsch
on the sabath. Potsdam, potsdorf potz gek und keine ende.
Bad case, bad as fake southern gentlemen tells you
everymorn that he is gentleman, and that he is not black.
Chinesemandarinorlaundryman   takes forgranted youwillsee he is
not BookerTWashington.

: : : : : :

Poem No. 2.

   Able Abel
Mounts dernier bateau   :
@¼%&:¼/?½ @¾) (&?;¼%@&%&&&&&
        ¼¼¼¼@¼% ;34%3

Little Review, Autumn 1921, detail. Reprinted by permission of the Ezra Pound Literary Property Trust and Faber and Faber Ltd. Copyright Ezra Pound 1921

YEAR 1 p. s. U.

1921-1922 Old Style

1921 O. S.
ZEUS

S		4	11	18	25
M		5	12	19	26
T		6	13	20	27
W		7	14	21	28
Th	1	8	15	22	29
F	2	9	16	23	30
S	3	10	17	24	31

Jan. 1922 O. S.
SATURN

S	1	8	15	22	29
M	2	9	16	23	30
T	3	10	17	24	31
W	4	11	18	25
Th	5	12	19	26
F	6	13	20	27
S	7	14	21	28

HERMES

S		5	12	19	26
M		6	13	20	27
T		7	14	21	28
W	1	8	15	22.
T	2	9	16	23
F	3	10	17	24
S	4	11	18	25

1921 O. S.
HEPHAISTOS

S		6	13	20	27
M		7	14	21	28
T	1	8	15	22	29
W	2	9	16	23	30
Th	3	10	17	24
F	4	11	18	25
S	5	12	19	26

MARS

S		5	12	19	26
M		6	13	20	27
T		7	14	21	28
W	1	8	15	22	29
Th	2	9	16	23	30
F	3	10	17	24	31
S	4	11	18	25

PHOEBUS

S	2	9	16	23	30
M	3	10	17	24
T	4	11	18	25
W	5	12	19	26
Th	6	13	20	27
F	7	14	21	28
S	1	8	15	22	29

KUPRIS

S		7	14	21	28
M	1	8	15	22	29
T	2	9	16	23	30
W	3	10	17	24	31
Th	4	11	18	25
F	5	12	19	26
S	6	13	20	27

ISIS

HORUS

INCIPIT

DEMETER

S	1	8	15	22	29
M	2	9	16	23	30
T	3	10	17	24	31
W	4	11	18	25
Th	5	12	19	26
F	6	13	20	27
S	7	14	21	28

HESTIA

S		6	13	20	27
M		7	14	21	28
T	1	8	15	22	29
W	2	9	16	23	30
Th	3	10	17	24	31
F	4	11	18	25
S	5	12	19	26

ATHENE

S		2	9	16	23	30
M		3	10	17	24	31
T		4	11	18	25
W		5	12	19	26
Th		6	13	20	27
F		7	14	21	28
S	1	8	15	22	29

ARTEMIS

S		3	10	17	24
M		4	11	18	25
T		5	12	19	26
W		6	13	20	27
Th		7	14	21	28
F	1	8	15	22	29
S	2	9	16	23	30

JUNO

S		4	11	18	25
M		5	12	19	26
T		6	13	20	27
W		7	14	21	28
Th	1	8	15	22	29
F	2	9	16	23	30
S	3	10	17	24

THE LITTLE REVIEW CALENDAR

The Little Review, Spring 1922

In early 1922, having now fallen out with Tzara and been reconciled with Breton, Picabia put together in Saint-Raphaël with the help of 'Christian' a tract, *La Pomme de Pins*, in support of the Congrès de Paris, called by Breton to draw up a 'balance sheet of the modern spirit'.[92] Amongst aphorisms and items of information printed at angles and in a wide variety of typefaces, is the salutation 'Bonjour Pound'. At this time also Pound's name is found amongst the Dada 'elect',[93] along with that of the Rumanian sculptor, Constantin Brancusi (1876–1957).

Pound and Brancusi were both guests at Picabia's New Year's Eve celebrations in 1921.[94] Brancusi had long known Marcel Duchamp, and like Picabia had been associated with the Stieglitz circle in New York.[95] He was one of the signatories of *La Pomme de Pins* in 1922.[96]

It has been argued that his friendship with Duchamp influenced Brancusi, and that certain of his humorous works, and those involving found objects and assemblage, show a congruity with Dada practices.[97] It was not these works, however, but his more conventional sculpture which seems to have interested Pound. That what might be called a Dadaist disregard or impatience could complement, for Brancusi as it did for Pound, a much more serene intention is suggested by one of the sculptor's remarks quoted by Pound in 1937: 'ONE OF THOSE DAYS WHEN I WOULD NOT HAVE GIVEN FIFTEEN MINUTES OF MY TIME FOR ANYTHING UNDER HEAVEN.'[98]

La Pomme de Pins, 25 February 1922

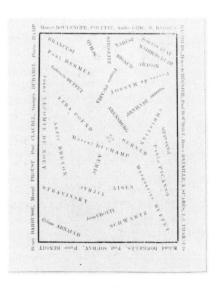

Plus de Cubisme, March 1922

II

In Paris Pound had become friendly with Brancusi, occasionally visiting his studio and sometimes being invited to a meal cooked by the sculptor.[99] Like Brancusi, Pound was a maker of his own furniture,[100] and Ford Madox Ford recalled in later years that 'As sculptor Ezra was of the school of Brancusi. He acquired pieces of stone as nearly egg-shaped as possible, hit them with hammers and then laid them about on the floor.'[101]

In April 1921 Pound was planning to 'start off with twenty Brancusis to get a new note' into *The Little Review*.[102] Whilst he was also planning special numbers of the magazine on Wyndham Lewis, Picasso and Picabia – and the unrealised book on *Four Modern Artists* – he had none of the doubts about Brancusi's art that he had at first about Picabia: 'From what I have seen I think he [Brancusi] is by far the best sculptor here. Picabia is alive, but as a thinker, regarding his painting in retrospect.'[103]

The same letter to John Quinn almost concedes William Carlos Williams's point about his taste in painting, with Pound declaring, 'I am more interested in literature and music than in painting . . .' Yet we have already touched on how his understanding of Gaudier-Brzeska's work and his thoughts on the 'hardness' he wanted in literature fruitfully complemented one another. From Paris Pound wrote of Brancusi to Ford Madox Ford that 'He is doing what Gaudier might have done in thirty years time'.[104]

Pound's essay on the sculptor in the Autumn 1921 'Brancusi Number' of *The Little Review* takes as its starting point T. J. Everets's formulation, 'A work of art has in it no idea which is separable from the form', and finds 'nothing in vorticist formulae which contradicts the work of Brancusi', even if they will not wholly 'satisfy' him:

> in a world where so few people have yet dissociated form from representation, one may, or at least I may as well approach Brancusi via the formulations by Gaudier-Brzeska, or by myself in my study of Gaudier.[105]

Although he does not claim to have arrived at a complete understanding of Brancusi, he takes up the spirit of his remark to Ford:

> Gaudier had discriminated against beefy statues, he had given us a very definite appreciation of stone as stone; he had taught us to feel that the beauty of sculpture is inseparable from its material and that it inheres in the material. Brancusi was giving up the facile success of representative sculpture about the time Gaudier was giving up his baby-bottle; in many ways his difference from Gaudier is a difference merely of degree, he has had time to make statues where Gaudier had time only to make sketches; Gaudier had purged himself of

every kind of rhetoric he had noticed; Brancusi has detected more kinds of rhetoric and continued the process of purgation.

When verbally intelligible he is quite definite in the statement that whatever else art is, it is not '*crise des nerfs*'; that beauty is not grimaces and fortuitous gestures; that starting with an ideal of form one arrives at a mathematical exactitude of proportion, but *not by* mathematics.[106]

Pound saw the two sculptors in agreement in so far as they were concerned with the formal content of their art over and above representation. For his part Gaudier-Brzeska had met Brancusi at the Allied Artists exhibition in 1913,[107] and had praised him as a craftsman locked in struggle with his medium –

> The sculpture I admire is the work of master craftsmen. Every inch of the surface is won at the point of the chisel – every stroke of the hammer is a physical and mental effort . . . Brancusi's greatest pride is his consciousness of being an accomplished workman.[108]

– in terms which prefigure Pound's enthusiasm for the rigour of Gautier.

In his 'Vortex' in *Blast* 1 Gaudier had ranged Brancusi amongst 'WE the moderns: Epstein, Brancusi, Archipenko, Dunikowski, Modigliani, and myself, through the incessant struggle in the complex city, have likewise to expend much energy'.[109] This may lead us into the differences which Pound perceived between the two sculptors. For in his New York *Evening Post* article Pound described Brancusi as one 'who lives in his atelier as a Dordogne cavern sculptor may conceivably have lived in his rock-fissure, content to let the world "think" or not think in any way it likes,'[110] choosing to align him not, as Gaudier had done, with the artists of the contemporary vortex of the city, but rather with the first vortex which Gaudier had noted in *Blast*: 'The PALEOLITHIC VORTEX resulted in the decoration of the Dordogne caverns'.[111]

The 'peace and quiet'[112] which Pound found so remarkable in Brancusi's studio seems to have been connected in his mind with his sense that Brancusi was pursuing something altogether more essential and serene than the 'nerve crisis'[113] and bustle of the 'complex city'. (Pound had noted that Brancusi's 'metaphysic' was 'outside and unrelated' to Vorticism, whatever the formal analogies between him and Gaudier.[114]

> Brancusi, in so different a way from Proust, has created a world, or let us say Proust has created a somewhat stuffy social *milieu*, and Brancusi has created a universe, a *cielo*, a Platonic heaven full of pure and essential forms, and a cavern of a studio which is, in a very old sense, a temple of peace, of stillness, a refuge from the noise of motor traffic and the current advertisements.[115]

Brancusi at work in his studio, 1922
Cliché Brancusi, Musée National d'Art Moderne, Paris

Gaudier-Brzeska, Pound states, 'developed a sort of form-fugue or form sonata by a combination of forms'.[116] But he never had the time to repeat a composition.[117] Despite the debt owed by other sculptors, including Gaudier, to Brancusi's practice of cutting and finishing the stone himself,[118] Pound sees the latter as unique in his 'devotion to and research for an absolute formal beauty'.[119] In *The Cantos* and elsewhere Pound repeatedly cites in whole or part Brancusi's words: 'Toutes mes choses datent de quinze ans. Je peux commencer une chose nouvelle tous les jours, mais finir?'[120] He is refining his forms toward 'the sort of Platonic quintessence, let us say "that which is birdlike in all birds"'.[121]

To Brancusi's 'ovoids' Pound gives the 'interim label' of 'master-keys to the world of form – not "his" world of form, but as much as he has found of "the" world of form'.[122] 'In the case of the ovoid, I take it Brancusi is meditating upon pure form free from all terrestrial gravitation; form as free in its own life as the form of the analytical geometers . . .'[123] The titles of the 'ovoids' – 'Sleeping Muse',

Constantin Brancusi, 'Prometheus', 1912
Kettle's Yard, University of Cambridge

'Prometheus', 'New Born' – indicate a contemplation of creation and its sources.[124] Whereas Pound's *Little Review* essay on Brancusi begins with a strongly individualist conception of the artist – '"I carve a thesis in logic of the eternal beauty," writes Rémy de Gourmont . . . A man hurls himself toward the infinite and the works of art are his vestiges, his trace in the manifest' – Brancusi's effort was towards concealing the trace of his hand: 'A work of art should be like a perfect crime'.[125] As a later critic has said, because 'he was more interested in the abstract or absolute value of a form distinct from its manifestation in a given material', and was given to casting the same form in a range of materials, 'it is difficult to believe that he was much concerned with stone as a means of achieving a particular kind of form' – in the way Gaudier-Brzeska thought he was.[126]

Pound acknowledges that the 'polish' upon some of Brancusi's brass surfaces served the sculptor's desire for 'greater precision of the form', eliminating the 'accidentals' and 'imperfections'. Nevertheless, he insists that 'the contemplation of form or of formal beauty leading into the infinite must be dissociated from the dazzle of crystal.'[127] Whereas the 'dazzle' is hypnotic, or excites the unconscious, 'with ideal form in marble it is an approach to the infinite *by form*, by precisely the highest possible degree of consciousness of formal perfection'. Donald Davie has shown how, in *The Cantos*, the crystal represents the 'wooing into awareness, and the holding in awareness, of the *forma*' (and here too we may think of the 'glassy surface' where Picabia's thought moves). Above the crystal stands the 'jade': 'the

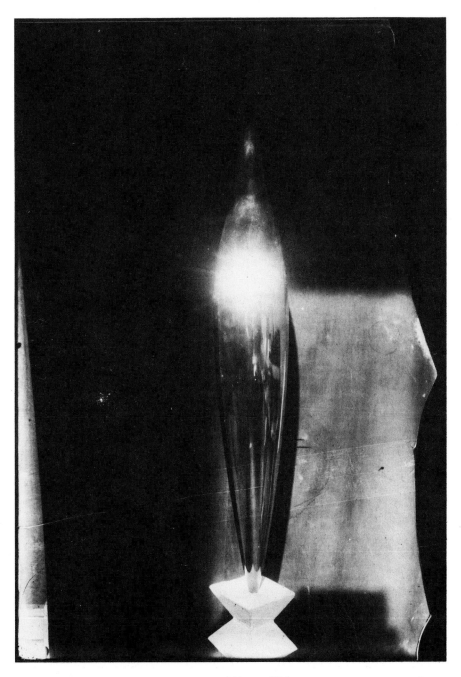

Constantin Brancusi, 'L'Oiseau d'Or', 1919–22
Cliché Brancusi, Musée National d'Art Moderne, Paris

art that comes of a marriage between the artist and nature is still, for Pound, superior to the art that comes by immaculate conception, self-generated'.[128] When it appears in *The Cantos*, the bird is emphatically Brancusi's:

> Brancusi's bird
> in the hollow of pine trunks
> or when the snow was like sea foam
> Twilit sky leaded with elm boughs.
> (Notes for CXVII et seq.)[129]

III

William Carlos Williams wrote that Ezra Pound 'missed the major impact of his age, the social impetus which underlies every effort on that front'.[130] In glossing Brancusi's love of perfection, his pursuit of the pure form, Pound alludes in *The Little Review* to 'absolute rhythm', an idea he had first advanced in 1910.[131] In this final section I should like to draw the idea of 'absolute rhythm' and what it suggests of the appreciation of speed and time, into the story of Pound's relationships with artists and his response to their machine art preoccupations in the second half of his stay in Paris. This will take us from the literary, the graphical and the sculptural, to painting, music and film, and should help us to weigh Williams's words.

After the New Year and the publication of the 'Paris Letter' on Brancusi considered above, and the distribution of *La Pomme de Pins* in Paris,[132] Pound left for Italy on 27 March 1922.[133] He returned to Paris early in July.[134] At about this time he met Ernest Hemingway, who in turn introduced him to William Bird and to Fernand Léger, Brancusi's 'special crony'.[135] William Bird had lately set up the Three Mountains Press on the Ile Saint-Louis, which in 1923 published Pound's autobiographical *Indiscretions*, and, in 1925, *A Draft of XVI Cantos*. Canto XVI quotes at some length from the war reminiscences of Fernand Léger.[136]

As we have seen, it was Pound's interest in Léger (1881–1955) which was singled out by William Carlos Williams as one of the proofs of his defective artistic judgement. Léger's experience of modern machinery in the Great War ('I was dazzled by the breech of a 75-millimetre gun'), and of ordinary men ('miners, navvies, workers in metal and wood'), the exuberant 'inventors of everyday poetic images', had made him reject the 'thoroughly abstract' pre-war preoccupation with conventional aesthetic subjects: 'Once I had got my teeth into that sort of reality I never let go of objects again.'[137]

In his 'Paris Letter' for *The Dial* of January 1923, Pound wrote of how Léger 'stopped painting and for some years puzzled over the problem of ideal machines, three-dimensional constructions having all the properties of machines save the ability to move or do work'.[138] Although this seems to be a misunderstanding, since Léger did not come to construct the machine sets for Marcel l'Herbier's film *L'Inhumaine* until later in 1923,[139] Pound is right that

> This is a perfectly serious aesthetic problem; Léger comes to a provisional answer in the negative, not convinced, but wondering whether the *objet*, the real machine, won't in the end be more interesting to look at, and *better aesthetically*.
>
> The struggle is interesting, at least as a symptom of sensitivity, and an evidence of his being aware of the much discussed and deplored gap between 'art and life' in our time.[140]

In the version of his Collège de France lecture on 'The Esthetics of the Machine' that was dedicated to Ezra Pound and published in the 'Exiles Number' (Pound's idea[141]) of *The Little Review* that spring, Léger himself outlined an aesthetic for 'our time'.[142] He believed in the beauty of the *objet*, but this was part of the idea of an absolute beauty unrelated to representation – an idea similar to that used by Pound in discussing Gaudier-Brzeska and Brancusi.

> I consider that plastic beauty in general is totally independent of sentimental descriptive or imitative values. Every object, picture, piece of architecture, or ornamental organization has a value in itself, strictly absolute, independent of anything it may happen to represent. Every object, created or manufactured, may carry in itself an intrinsic beauty just like all the phenomena of the natural order admired by the world, through all eternity.[143]

Léger maintains that there is no 'hierarchy of beauty',[144] of the kind which establishes the gap between museum art, what Pound called the bit of jade in a box, and the object in use:

> Beauty is everywhere . . . In the order of the pots and pans on the white wall of your kitchen more perhaps than in your eighteenth century salon or in the official museums. If you admit this type of esthetic judgement it is possible to reach an understanding of the nature of the beauty of machines.[145]

Pound had himself asserted that machines might possess a beauty of form, 'though the fact of this beauty is in itself offensive to the school of sentimental aesthetics'[146] (as it was offensive to Mauberley), and that the enjoyment of machines might be just as natural as the 'enjoyment of nature for its own sake' in the Renaissance.[147]

Léger now goes on to call for 'a union between the artisan and the artist',[148] for men 'able to consider the work of the artisan and of nature as first material'.[149] They must know 'how to arrange it, to absorb it', and not fall into the error of the 'School of Fine Arts' – the belief that the 'fine subject', whether natural or manufactured, can be copied: 'Although I tried personally in 1918 to catch in several pictures the equivalence of the beautiful mechanical object I always carefully avoided making a copy.'[150]

Ezra Pound, in his *Antheil and the Treatise on Harmony* of the following year, wrote, 'A painting of a machine is like a painting of a painting.'[151] In subsequently preparing a book on machine art, or art and machines, that was never finally produced, Pound had reservations about the ability of photography to capture machines similar to those he had about photographs of sculpture.[152] More particularly he stressed that the intrinsic beauty of machines lay in their moving parts and their pivots, where the energy was concentrated, whilst the static parts obeyed the laws of architecture.[153]

Léger found the 'School of Fine Arts' emphasis on copying the result of a misguided deference to the men of the Renaissance, who, in error, thought 'themselves superior to their predecessors the Primitives, in imitating natural forms instead of seeking their inner rhythm'.[154] What makes this of interest is that whereas the French text reads 'l'équivalence', here the *Little Review* version has 'inner rhythm'.[155] Whether or not Pound had a hand in the use of this phrase we perhaps cannot know, but as touched on above, Pound's own views on rhythm had begun to form over ten years earlier. It is in relation to Léger and to George Antheil that these ideas come to bear upon machine art. In the introduction to his translations of Cavalcanti in 1910 Pound declared his belief in 'an ultimate and absolute rhythm'. In poetry 'The perception of the intellect is given in the word, that of the emotions in the cadence. It is only, then, in perfect rhythm joined to the perfect word that the twofold vision can be recorded.'[156] But rhythm is 'absolute' not only in that it is necessary to the achievement of the fullest vision in a work of art, but also in another sense: it 'is perhaps the most primal of all things known to us'.[157] Ruth Heyman has made the following distinction – perhaps prompted by Ezra Pound – that 'Rhythm is in the year and its seasons recurrently flowing. Time is their marking off into days and hours.'[158]

To return to Pound's remarks on Brancusi, and to the Dantescan 'melody which most in-centres the soul', and the 'absolute rhythm' which is the sheer perfection of the art, it seems that this may be understood in two slightly different but complementary senses: firstly as the pulse of the artist's emotion in time with the rhythms of his world[159] – in a way which may illumine Pound's liking for Thomas Hardy's *Under the Greenwood Tree* – and secondly as the matching of the rhythm of the artist's experience to the art form to which it is best fitted.[160]

With regard to the rhythms not of the life of Mellstock village but of the city, Pound had written in his first month in Paris that

> The life of a village is narrative, you have not been there three weeks before you know that in the revolution et cetera, and when M. le Comte et cetera, and so forth. In a city the visual impressions succeed each other, overlap, overcross, they are 'cinematographic', but they are not a simple linear sequence.[161]

Léger gave his lecture on 'L'Esthétique de la Machine' at the Collège de France on 1 June 1923. Accompanying it were a small exhibition of works by 'the artisans of the machine', and a screening of hitherto unshown reels from Abel Gance's film *La Roue*.[162] Léger had been aware of the creative possibilities of film as early as 1918–19, chiefly through his friendship with the simultanist poet Blaise Cendrars (1887–1961), who worked with Abel Gance,[163] and whose *L'ABC du Cinéma* discussed the use of the cut in film and the possibility of increasing the viewer's awareness of objects by isolating them out of context and in close-up.[164]

Léger's work on Cendrars's two books *J'ai Tué* (1918) and *La Fin du monde filmée par l'Ange Notre-Dame* (1919) was formative in the development of his own simultanist style in painting in the years immediately following the Great War.[165] In the second of these books, Léger goes beyond simultanism in the illustrations themselves – using disruptive 'cutting' effects and 'close-ups' of recognisable objects – to a simultanist interpenetration of the visual elements and the text itself, with the former even at times shaped by the latter in a way which recalls Apollinaire and the calligram.[166]

The arrangement of Pound's cantos across as well as down the page, in compliance with the demands of the broken pentameter and of the 'cut' from culture to culture, tends to create them in some sense as plastic objects even before the entrance of a more obviously pictorial element with the ideograms later in *The Cantos*.[167] There is, however, a distinction to draw between poetry arranged on the page so as to mimic exterior space – or which, rivalling painting, offers 'des possibilités de la lecture simultanée'[168] – and that which is set out in accord with its own space. At all events, Pound was certainly aware of Cendrars's poetry, which so far as is possible to tell from his review notices he seems to have considered worthy of attention.[169]

> Léger himself did not yet turn to the making of films, but his new simultanist painting aligned itself closely with the new progressive simultanism of the cinema, it was as much a cinematic as a literary style, and behind both its cinematic and its literary qualities lay the creative support of Cendrars.[170]

Léger did, however, have a hand, with Cendrars, in the making of Gance's *La*

Roue between 1919 and 1921.[171] In a review published in *Comoedia*,[172] Léger praised 'the first three sections' of the film, 'where the mechanical element plays a major rôle' in this story of a railway mechanic bringing up an orphan girl. In these first sections (the result of Cendrars's editing) Léger considered that the director had 'elevated the art of film to the plane of the plastic arts', its rightful place, freeing it from the erroneous imitation of the theatre, from the descriptive and the sentimental. The 'plastic' qualities Léger focused on were chiefly the use of close-up, fragmentation and speed. More particularly these are manifested in 'the balance of still and moving parts' (as 'a still figure on a machine that is moving'), and the 'interplay' of abstract or geometrical forms with each other and with parts of the body ('his eye, his hand, his finger, his fingernail'), given sudden clarity by their isolation and magnification.

Ezra Pound also reviewed *La Roue*, in February 1923.[173] He does not mention the director, but gives Blaise Cendrars the credit for the 'interesting moments' and those 'effects' in the film 'which belong, perhaps, only to the cinema'. The review somewhat unconfidently echoes Léger's.

> At least for the sake of argument we can admit that they [the effects] are essentially cinematographic, and not a mere travesty and degradation of some other art. The bits of machinery, the varying speeds, the tricks of the reproducing machine are admirably exploited, according to pictorial concepts derived from contemporary abstract painters. The thing takes place on the railway, the driving wheels of the locomotive, et cetera, et cetera, the composition of the photos of the actual machinery, are interesting . . .

Although he commented unfavourably on the French 'lack of plot', he also appreciated the way in which sentiment detracted from the composition and visual effects. If the film itself had had 'everything possible' done for it by way of lurid and sensational publicity material to exploit it, to 'make art a commercial proposition', its qualities failed to overcome Pound's sense that film was not itself a true art – an art in which 'tricks' were 'exploited' was not an art produced out of engagement with an unyielding material such that it would 'endure'.

Christopher Green has given a thorough survey of the extent to which Léger's notions of the 'pure' art of film liberated from the theatre, and the use of isolation, fragmentation, enlargement and movement, were all ideas held in common by film-makers and critics at the time.[174] In particular, René Clair wrote on the movement of images in relation to one another. By which, Green writes,

> He means the rhythm created by the succession of images, each projected for differing lengths of time, the rhythm created by cutting from one image to another at a measured speed – the kind of movement for which *La Roue* was commonly taken as *the* exemplar.[175]

Jean Epstein also 'dwelt on the measured cutting from image to image as key to rhythm',[176] and in Clair's review of Epstein's *Coeur fidèle* he wrote on the question of rhythm, and how the film-maker uses 'images recalled' in the way that a poet might use 'assonance or rhyme'.[177]

Fernand Léger finally clarified his approach to film when he came to make his own *Ballet mécanique* in late 1923 and early 1924.[178] At this time he was also designing and constructing the laboratory sets with moving machine parts for Marcel l'Herbier's film about a concert singer, the 'inhuman one', *L'Inhumaine*.[179] L'Herbier's film contains a riot scene shot at a specially arranged concert given by George Antheil, who did not know that cameras had been installed in the theatre.[180] Amongst other notables in the rioting audience were James Joyce, Ezra Pound and Man Ray.[181]

George Antheil (1900–1959) was a young American pianist and composer who, after meeting Pound in the summer of 1923, helped him to edit his opera *Le Testament de Villon* and participated in concerts of Pound's violin music.[182] Pound wrote a number of articles on Antheil, some of which found their way into his *Antheil and the Treatise on Harmony*, published by William Bird in 1924. According to Antheil, the piece which really did cause bedlam at the concert filmed for

George Antheil, photograph by Man Ray

[109]

L'Inhumaine was his 'Mechanisms'. Soon after this he began 'working on a new piece, to be called *Ballet mécanique*' (a title used by Picabia for the cover illustration of *391*, no.7 in 1917), and to have 'a motion-picture accompaniment'.[183]

Pound seems to have put Antheil in touch with the American cameraman and director Dudley Murphy,[184] with whom that year Pound may already have considered making a vortographic film.[185] Pound brought Antheil and Murphy together with Léger,[186] who financed the film[187] and, with Murphy, suggested images, collaborated at the editing stage when the film was given its rhythmic form, and was the overall 'coordinator of the film's creation'.[188] *Ballet mécanique* was not, as Pound described *La Roue*, a film for 'the million'. In an article published in *The Little Review* just after Ezra Pound's name ceased to appear on the masthead, Léger described it as having 'No scenario – Reactions of rhythmic images, that is all'.[189] Those images are 'Objects . . . the most usual': 'Figures, fragments of figures, mechanical fragments, metals, manufactured objects . . .' Léger declared that the film 'is objective, realistic and in no way abstract', for to him the isolated object or detail was 'a personality'. Interactions of 'contrasted or analogous'[190] images and repetitions contributed to this end.

Léger describes the images as 'rhythmic'; overall they were arranged in rhythmic sequences, with rhythm and speed as the structural principles of the film.

> Two coefficients of interest upon which the film is constructed:
> The variation of the speeds of projection:
> The rhythm of these speeds.

Fernand Léger, 'Ballet mécanique', 1923–4
still copyright Raymond Rohauer Collection

The 'rhythmic use of cutting'[191] also often transformed static into dynamic images. Léger himself acknowledged a significant debt both in the direction of the rhythmic image and of the presentation of the object with a 'minimum of perspective': 'An important contribution due to a technical novelty of Mr Murphy and Mr Ezra Pound – the multiple transformation of the projected image.' This novelty was related to the technique – developed in London by Pound and the photographer Alvin Langdon Coburn (see pp.69 – 72 of this catalogue) – for the multiplication and fragmentation of the photographic image by means of pieces of glass arranged into a kaleidoscope or prism placed before the lens. The effect of this device when applied to film in *Ballet mécanique* is well described by Standish Lawder:

By holding a prism over the lens, the camera's field of vision is shattered in such a way that forms appear to overlap and interpenetrate each other. The device suited Léger's mode of vision to perfection, for, through a prism, perspective was totally destroyed and space flattened. Moreover, any movement of an object photographed in this manner took on a curiously jerky and mechanical quality. This happens because the same object is seen simultaneously in several different positions on the screen, and each optically replicated and overlaid image performs the same movement in mechanical unison with all its other identical images.

For instance . . . we see an arrangement of highly reflective Christmas tree ornaments against a background of geometric elements. Through prismatic fracturing, their number is multiplied on the screen and, when set in motion, the elements of this truly Cubist composition move about in syncopated rhythm as if linked together by invisible tie-rods . . .[192]

George Antheil's own *Ballet mécanique*, which Léger described as 'a musically synchronised adaptation' for the film, ultimately developed separately. It was given its première, with some décor by Léger, on 19 June 1926, ten days before that of Pound's opera from Villon.[193] If Pound felt, as in the review of *La Roue*, that film possessed insufficient powers of 'endurance', and was satisfied by Gance's film that the cinema was 'no use as an art', it is from his reviews of Antheil's première and his book on the composer that we may receive the clearest idea of Pound's opinion on the most suitable medium for machine art – in which the pianola is freed from the ignominy it shared with the 'kinema' in 'Hugh Selwyn Mauberley'. As a necessary feature of modern experience, machines should properly be one of the concerns of art:

Machines are now a part of life, it is proper that men should feel something about them; there would be something weak about art if it couldn't deal with this new content.[194]

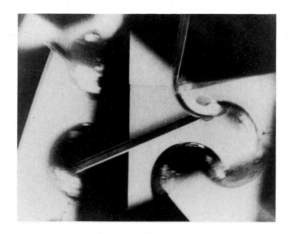

Fernand Léger, 'Ballet mécanique', 1923–4
still copyright Raymond Rohauer Collection

He speaks of 'art', not 'an art', and the assumption that music is the one 'most fit to express the fine quality of machines' is given sense by the 'return to the vorticist demands':

'Every concept, every emotion presents itself to the vivid consciousness in some primary form, it belongs to the art of that form.'
I am inclined to think that machines acting in time-space, and hardly existing save when in action, belong chiefly to an art acting in time-space; at any rate Antheil has used them, effectively.[195]

It has been Antheil's contribution to re-emphasise the 'horizontal' successive quality of time in music, over harmony, the 'static'.[196] The special quality of machines, what marks them out, is movement and rhythm. Pound had written that 'A rhythm unit is a shape; it exists like the keel-line of a yacht, or the lines of an automobile engine, for a definite purpose, and should exist with an efficiency as definite as that which we find in yachts and automobiles.' Later that 'shape' became assimilated also to the sculptural, rhythm being 'a form cut into TIME, as a design is determined SPACE',[197] but

Machines are musical. I doubt if they are even very pictorial or sculptural, they have form, but their distinction is not in form, it is in their movement and energy; reduced to sculptural stasis they lose *raison d'être*, as if their essence.[198]

With Antheil's *Ballet mécanique* Pound identifies 'a new musical act; a new grip on life by the art'.[199]

Christopher Green speculates that it was Léger's first-hand experience of the rhythmic, dynamic art of film that showed him the 'essentially static nature of the immobile arts, most obviously of all easel-painting', and that it may have been no coincidence that at the same time as he was becoming involved in film he was moving in his painting 'decisively toward the stable easel-painting principles of his "call to order"'.[200] The development of Pound's argument in his essay on Léger written in 1922, also takes us from the 'dynamic' to the stable – to Pound's admiration for artists willing to work, not in the easily 'vendible' medium of the easel-painting, but on an architectural scale.

The paragraph in Pound's essay which ends on the 'evidence of [Léger's] being aware of the . . . gap between "art and life" in our time' is followed by:

> Léger returns to painting and finds the easel picture a constriction. Many of his designs only become effective when one imagines them forty feet by sixty, instead of the twelve by fifteen demanded by studio limits. Ghirlandaio wanted to paint the town walls of Florence. Léger would be perfectly happy doing the outside of a railway terminal, or probably doing an ad on the slab side of a skyscraper.[201]

In February of 1923 the sculptor Joseph Csaky's architectural arrangement of shaped panels painted by Léger was shown at the Salon des Indépendants.[202] The powerfully coloured decorations were intended for both the inside and the outside of an imaginary building.[203] This seems to be the first real evidence of Léger's painting for architecture, and it is possible that Léger was preparing these panels at the end of 1922 when Pound wrote his article.[204] The painter's L'Architecture of 1923 now had as its main theme the polychromatic architecture that had been anticipated in the Paysages animés of 1921.[205] Christopher Green suggests that the 1923 painting may express Léger's 'strengthened faith' in the idea of the outsides of buildings transformed by brightly coloured paint.[206] It was, however, in late 1923 that Léger, influenced by Van Doesburg, actually began to move away from a dynamism that worked against the architecture it decorated, and in the direction Pound's article goes on to suggest: towards 'an harmonious alliance between painter and architect' – realised in his later collaborations with Le Corbusier and Mallet-Stevens – in which the mural was a complementary part of the architecture itself.[207]

The sort of rapid shift Pound makes, as between Léger and Ghirlandaio, making comparisons across time, is as much a feature of The Cantos as of his prose. When the notice 'Obit Picabia 2. Dec. '53' occurs amidst elements of American history and money theory (Canto LXXXIX),[208] it is part of the weave of time and space in the poem. In the prose such broad analogies may be insightful and stimulating, both with regard to the artists themselves and to Pound's own work. Pound's interest in artists as individuals, in the character or personality from which their work proceeds, together with his ability to take them on as masks, also causes time to fall away. This obscures another sort of 'gap between "art and life"', a gap Pound was well aware of, the gap between live and dead artists, and, more important, between the different social and economic circumstances in which they live. That is to say that Pound's conception of art contains a view of life that was not necessarily in tune with present fact.

As we have seen in this essay, Pound's art has room for, on the one hand, a care for the object, for clarity of expression and perfection of form – virtues which, in their purest expression as embodied in art, give access to a higher sphere – as in the case of Brancusi – and on the other a polemical or satirical side. The two are often complementary – Pound could admire Léger, the artist concerned with the object, and in particular the real machine, and also Picabia, in whose art the machine is used to 'dissociate', to 'satirise'. The formal and the satirical may work together in trying to close the gap between the values of art and the values of modern life. The terminology responds to this. Pound admired Picabia's satirical 'nettoyage' because it sought to clear out all that stood in the way of the 'sense of form' he praised Brancusi for, a sense of form which 'ought to be as general as the sense of refreshment after a bath'.[209] As in *The Cantos*, water and stone are close.

The juxtaposition of Léger and Ghirlandaio is the first stroke in Pound's discussion in the 1922 essay of the social and economic conditions under which the artist works, territory already familiar from the satire of *Hugh Selwyn Mauberley*. Pound did not talk of the decline of the Paris Vortex as he had of that in London, but the same evils to his mind seem to have afflicted both halves of the 'double city of London and Paris'.[210]

Fernand Léger, 'L'Architecture', 1923 *Private Collection*

Through it all is the elegy, the lament that we lack a 'chef d'orchestre'; that painting ought to be a part of architecture; that there is no place for painting or sculpture in modern life; that painters make innumerable scraps of paper. This is true. The stuff is vendible or non-vendible: . . .

Pound's attempt to relocate art in modern life by proposing Antheil's *Ballet mécanique* as a model for the orchestration of the shop floor only pointed up how out of touch he was with industrial conditions.[211] The moral drawn from the following anecdote may well leave us with a similar sense of unreality:

A rising painter said to me last week, 'In a few years my worst competitors [in the job of making a living] will be the people who have bought my early work.' This bogy did not weigh on the man who painted his masterpiece on an irremovable wall. He could *afford* to work for his bare board and keep.

Although Pound was dismissive, in a passage strongly reminiscent of one of Marinetti's pre-war London lectures, of Ruskin's 'pastoral retrogression',[212] the Quattrocento he turns to in the essay on Léger does in fact constitute a kind of pastoral, as the word 'elegy' suggests, in which a natural order regulated relationships between artists and between them and the *chef d'orchestre*. That this was not merely a late growth, but may be viewed as the natural order upon which the satirical 'nettoyage' of the earlier Paris years was premised is suggested by Pound's essay on Dolmetsch of 1918:

Is it that nature can, in fact, only produce a certain number of vortices? That the quattrocento shines out because the vortices of social power coincided with the vortices of creative intelligence? And that when these vortices do not coincide we have an age of 'art in strange corners' . . .? Is it that real democracy can only exist under feudal conditions, when no man fears to recognise creative skill in his neighbour?[213]

It has been suggested that Ezra Pound left Paris both because of the cliquishness of the art world[214] – a cliquishness that may have made him feel left out, for he was not always there the *chef d'orchestre* he had been in London – and because of his interest in developments in Italy,[215] where he had been researching the Malatesta Cantos. The essay on Léger had begun: 'Experimentalism leaves perhaps more modes than men desirous of perfecting any one mode.' This may serve as a fitting note on which to conclude this account of Pound's activities in Paris before his departure for Italy, where he had found the values he admired in the art of the past, and where he would work for their embodiment in the present, in *The Cantos*.

Notes

1 'Harold Monro', *The Criterion* (July 1932), p.590.
2 *The Penguin Book of French Verse 3, The Nineteenth Century*, ed. Anthony Hartley (Harmondsworth, 1963), pp.137–9.
3 'The hard and soft in French poetry', *Literary Essays of Ezra Pound*, ed. T. S. Eliot (London, 1954), p.285.
4 John J. Espey, *Ezra Pound's 'Mauberley', a study in composition* (London, 1955), pp.27–8.
5 *Gaudier-Brzeska: A Memoir* (New York, 1970), pp.19, 107.
6 'E.P. Ode pour l'élection de son sépulcre', III, *Ezra Pound, Collected Shorter Poems* (London, 1984), p.189.
7 *Gaudier*, p.43.
8 'E.P. Ode pour l'élection de son sépulcre', II, p.188.
9 'Mauberley', *Collected Shorter Poems*, p.198.
10 *Gaudier*, p.50.
11 'The hard and soft in French poetry', p.285.
12 '"The age demanded"', *Collected Shorter Poems*, p.201.
13 *Gaudier*, p.114. 'For when words cease to cling close to things, kingdoms fall, empires wane and diminish.'
14 *Ibid.*, pp.26, 116.
15 '... speculation as to ... whether in one's anthropo- and gunaikological passion one were wise to leave London itself – with possibly a parenthetical Paris as occasional watch-tower and alternating exotic mica salis –', Ezra Pound, *Indiscretions, or Une Revue de Deux Mondes* (Paris, 1923), pp.9–10.
16 Noel Stock, *The Life of Ezra Pound* (Harmondsworth, 1985), p.288.
17 *Ibid.*, pp.290, 292.
18 'The Island of Paris: a letter', *The Dial* (October 1920), p.406.
19 Pound recalled how 'Somewhere about 1920 Louis Aragon sat on my decrepit sofa in the Hôtel de l'Elysée and told me about suicide. He admired it, programmatically.' Ezra Pound, 'René Crevel', *The Criterion* (October 1938–January 1939), p.228.
20 *The Dial* (October 1920), pp.407–8.
21 George Heard Hamilton, *Painting and Sculpture in Europe, 1880–1940* (Harmondsworth, 1967), p.241. See also

William A. Camfield, *Francis Picabia, His Art, Life and Times* (Princeton, NJ, 1979), p.117 and n.3.
22 Hamilton, p.239. There is more than one account of the origins and discovery of the word.
23 Marc le Bot, *Francis Picabia et la crise des valeurs figuratives, 1900–1925* (Paris, 1968), p.194.
24 *Ibid.*
25 Hamilton, p.241; Camfield, *Francis Picabia*, p.25. It 'haunted' Breton.
26 Hamilton, p.254.
27 'The Curse', *The Apple (of Beauty and Discord)* (January 1920), p.22.
28 'The New Sculpture', *The Egoist* (16 February 1914), p.68.
29 *Littérature*, 16, 1er série (September–October 1920), reprinted in Andrew Clearfield, 'Pound, Paris and Dada', *Paideuma*, 7, Appendix 6, p.140.
30 *Gaudier*, pp.103, 122.
31 'Praefatio ad lectorem electum', *The Spirit of Romance* (New York, 1968), p.5.
32 'French Poets', *Make it New* (London, 1934), p.223.
33 *Ibid.*, p.171.
34 'The Island of Paris', p.409.
35 'The hard and soft in French poetry', pp.288–9; 'French Poets', p.216.
36 *Gaudier*, p.119. See also Pound's letter to John Quinn from Paris, 21 May 1921: 'at any rate the air is cleaner here than in London; and there are at least a handful of people who aren't in moribund state of mind' (*Ezra Pound and the Visual Arts*, ed. Harriet Zinnes (New York, 1980), p.246).
37 'The Island of Paris', p.411.
38 Clearfield, 'Pound, Paris and Dada', pp.128–9. See for instance, *The Dial* (January 1921), p.110, re Cocteau's 'perceptive intelligence'.
39 See 'Axiomata' (*The New Age*, January 1921), *Selected Prose, 1909–65*, ed. William Cookson (London, 1973), p.52; see also Stock, p.294, and Pound's letter to Quinn, 21 May 1921 (see n.36 above).
40 Stock, p.295.
41 Camfield, *Francis Picabia*, p.157 and n.25; Michel Sanouillet, *Dada à Paris* (Paris, 1965), pp.248, 268.
42 Stock, p.298.
43 *The Cantos*, 3rd edn (London, 1975), p.510.
44 'Christian', 'Annales du Pélican', *Cahiers*

Dada Surréalisme, 2 (1968), pp.190, 193.

45 Y. Poupard-Lieussou, 'Christian, "Le Pérégrin dans l'ombre"', *Cahiers Dada Surréalisme*, 3 (1969) p.21. The Pounds left London for Paris and the South of France in May 1919 (Stock, p.281). On 'Christian' and Picabia, see Camfield, *Francis Picabia*, p.180 n.57; Sanouillet, pp.339, 517, 519, 327 n.3.

46 'Christian', 'Annales du Pélican', p.193.

47 *Pound/Ford . . . The Correspondence between Ezra Pound and Ford Madox Ford*, ed. B. Lindberg-Seyersted (London, 1982), p.56. Picabia was seriously ill in the spring of 1921, but his whereabouts at this time are uncertain (Le Bot, p.195).

48 Camfield, *Francis Picabia*, p.160 n.36; Clearfield, p.120. [Fond Doucet letter A-1-1 (4) no.406.] Margaret Anderson, the magazine's editor, may also have had a hand in the appointment, remembering the activities of Dada in New York – see Sanouillet, p.362 and n.2.

49 Letters to Quinn, 10 March 1916 (Zinnes, p.280); 13 July 1916 (*ibid.*, p.239); 24 January 1917 (*ibid.*, p.281). *The New Age*, 27 March 1919 (*ibid.*, p.108).

50 *Selected Letters of Ezra Pound, 1907–1941*, ed. D. D. Paige (London, 1980), p.176.

51 Zinnes, p.246.

52 Quoted in William Marling, *William Carlos Williams and the Painters, 1909–1923* (Athens, Ohio, 1982), p.30.

53 Letter to Wyndham Lewis, 27 April 1921 (Zinnes, p.282).

54 Letter to John Quinn, 21 May 1921 (*ibid.*, p.246): '. . . regarding his painting in retrospect. Though I think he has done some good pictures at one time or another.'

55 *Ibid.*, p.282.

56 Le Bot, p.191.

57 See Camfield, *Francis Picabia*; also his 'The Machinist Style of Francis Picabia', *Art Bulletin*, 48 (1966), pp.309–22.

58 For a brief summary of other strands in his work during the period, see Le Bot, p.193.

59 Dawn Ades, *Dada and Surrealism Reviewed* (London, 1978), p.145; Hamilton, pp.243, 255.

60 Ezra Pound, 'Literature abroad, Parisian literature', *Literary Review*, New York *Evening Post*, 13 August 1921, p.7.

61 *The Dial*, 71 (October 1921), p.458.

62 *Ibid.*, pp.457–8.

63 Theo Van Doesburg, *Mécano*, 1–4/5 (Leiden, 1922–3; Vaduz, 1979); *Mécano*,

1 (September 1922).

64 *Ibid.*, introduction by J. Leering.

65 The name I. K. Bonset was first used in the pages of *De Stijl* in May 1920, see Jane Beckett, 'Dada, Van Doesburg and De Stijl', ed. Richard Sheppard, *Dada, Studies of a Movement* (Chalfont St Giles, 1980), pp.2–3.

66 *Ibid.*, p.2, etc.

67 Van Doesburg, quoted in Joost Baljeu, *Theo Van Doesburg* (New York, 1974), p.39.

68 Van Doesburg's homage to Ruskin here further draws the men together, suggesting the direction, or social impetus, of their thought. For Ezra Pound and Ruskin, see Guy Davenport, 'The house that Jack built', *The Geography of the Imagination* (San Francisco, 1981), p.46.

69 *Cantos*, p.438.

70 In retrospect on Paris Pound seems to have considered Dada 'the next phase' on from *Blast* (*Guide to Kulchur*, New York, 1968, p.95; 'D'Artagnan twenty years after', *Selected Prose*, p.428), and identified a line of descent running from *Blast* to Cocteau (*ibid.*) It was Picabia's mental activities ('D'Artagnan', p.428), his brilliance (*Guide to Kulchur*, pp.84, 105) to which Pound gave the central place in Dada. He wrote of the 'excitement of mental peril which accompanied Francis Picabia' ('D'Artagnan', p.429). These terms are close to those we shall see in Pound's *Little Review* essay on Brancusi, concerning the brilliant crystal (and we may think of the 'glassy surface' where Picabia's thought moves), whose contemplation results in an 'excitement of the "subconscious" or unconscious'. This is less than, but may also precede, the conscious apprehension of form:

> Picabia got hold of an instrument which cleared out whole racks full of rubbish . . . That anyone shd [*sic*] have tried to use Picabia's acid for building stone, shows only the ineradicable desire of second-rate minds to exploit things they have not comprehended. After Dada there came a totally different constructive movement (*Guide to Kulchur*, pp.87–8).

71 Ades, p.146.

72 *Ibid.*

73 *Ibid.*

74 Camfield, *Francis Picabia*, p.163.

75 'For a new paideuma', *Selected Prose*, p.257.

76 Camfield, *Francis Picabia*, p.163; for

'Christian's' links with the magazine, see Poupard-Lieussou, '"Christian", le Pérégrin dans l'ombre', p.21.

77 Camfield, p.165; Clearfield, Appendices 1–3.

78 *Ça Ira*, ed. Jacques Antoine (Paris, 1973), p.110; on Pansaers, Picabia and *Ça Ira* see Rik Sauwen, 'L'Esprit Dada en Belgique', *Cahiers Dada Surréalisme*, 4 (1970), p.119. I am grateful to Marc Dachy for information concerning the planned publication of *Biblioquet* in December 1921, which was to have included work by Pound, Picabia, Brancusi and Clement Pansaers, the Belgian Dadaist who knew 'Christian'. See *Dada-Constructivism* (London, 1984), p.114.

79 Clearfield, p.120 and n.29; the remark also appears in 'Christian's' memoir, 'In the minor key of an epoch', *The Little Review* (Winter, 1922), p.30.

80 Lindberg-Seyersted, p.58. Alan Young, *Dada and After, Extremist Modernism and English Literature* (Manchester, 1981), p.85, argued (in response to Clearfield, pp.119–20), that the poem is Picabia's doing – although a letter at Fond-Doucet (A-1-1(7) no.26) may suggest the contrary.

81 Serge Fauchereau, *Expressionisme, dada, surréalisme et autres ismes* (Paris, 1976), p.210; Sanouillet, p.139.

82 Edmund Wilson, *To the Finland Station* (London, 1972), pp.71–2.

83 J.P. Stern, *Hitler: The Führer and the People* (London, 1984), p.41.

84 *Ibid.*

85 *Selected Prose*, p.394.

86 Denis Mack Smith, *Mussolini* (London, 1983), p.146; Ezra Pound, letter to the editor, *The Criterion* (January 1935), p.304; Peter Nicholls, *Ezra Pound, Politics, Economics and Writing* (London, 1984), p.96.

87 'Abel Sanders' also contributed a note on 'Sculpshure' to *The Little Review*, (January–March 1921), p.47.

88 Clearfield, pp.121–2, reprinted at *ibid.*, Appendix IV.

89 Clearfield, Appendix V; Ades, p.147.

90 'D'Artagnan', p.429.

91 See Clearfield, p.122; Stock, p.311; William C. Wees, *Vorticism and the English Avant-Garde* (Toronto, 1972), p.160. Pound and Picabia seem to have shared an interest in the astronomical and the scientific – see Camfield, *Francis Picabia*,

p.321 on the sources of Picabia's imagery. Compare Picabia's 'Astrolabe' and Pound's rose in the iron filings.

92 'Christian', 'Annales du Pélican', p.194; Ades, p.148.

93 Sanouillet, p.339.

94 Camfield, *Francis Picabia*, p.171.

95 Edith Balas, 'Brancusi, Duchamp and Dada', *Gazette des Beaux Arts*, 95 (1980), pp.165–74; Sidney Geist, 'Brancusi, the Meyers, and *Portrait of Mrs Eugene Meyer Jr*', *Studies in the History of Art*, 6 (1974), pp.189–212.

96 Sanouillet, p.339; Balas, 'Brancusi, Duchamp and Dada', p.173.

97 See Balas, 'Brancusi, Duchamp and Dada'.

98 *Selected Prose*, p.253.

99 Stock, p.301.

100 *Ibid.*, p.299; on Brancusi and furniture see Balas, 'Brancusi, Duchamp and Dada'.

101 Ford Madox Ford, *Memories and Impressions* (Harmondsworth, 1979), p.326.

102 Letter to Wyndham Lewis, 27 April 1921 (Zinnes, p.282).

103 Letter to John Quinn, 21 March 1921 (Zinnes, p.246).

104 Letter to Ford Madox Ford, August 1921 (Lindberg-Seyersted, p.61).

105 'Brancusi', *Literary Essays*, p.441.

106 *Ibid.*, p.442.

107 Wees, p.135.

108 Gaudier-Brzeska's review of the Allied Artists' Association, *Gaudier*, p.31.

109 'Vortex. Gaudier-Brzeska', *Blast 1* (1914) (Santa Barbara, 1981), p.158.

110 See n.60 above.

111 See *Blast 1*, p.155.

112 Stock, p.301.

113 'Paris Letter', *The Dial* (January 1922) (Zinnes, p.171).

114 'Brancusi', *Literary Essays*, p.444.

115 'Paris Letter' (Zinnes, p.172).

116 'Brancusi', p.442.

117 Zinnes, p.172.

118 Hamilton, p.310.

119 Zinnes, p.171.

120 cf. Cantos LXXXVI and XCVII, *Cantos*, pp.560 and 677; *Prolegomena* (Var, 1932).

121 Zinnes, p.172.

122 'Brancusi', p.443.

123 *Ibid.*, p.444.

124 Hamilton, pp.309–10.

125 Quoted at Sidney Geist, 'Brancusi, the Meyers, and *Portrait of Mrs Eugene Meyer, Jr*', *Studies in the History of Art* (1974), p.209.

126 Hamilton, p.510. There is a further

difference here from Vorticist habits of work in so far as Pound sees Brancusi's forms as conceived so as to be beautiful from whatever angle they may be seen – as one might expect of a Platonic form – however violently they are upset. *Literary Essays*, pp.443–4.

127 'Brancusi', p.444.

128 Donald Davie, *Ezra Pound, Poet as Sculptor* (London, 1965), pp.220ff., 231–2.

129 *Cantos*, p.801.

130 Quoted at Marling, p.30.

131 *The Translations of Ezra Pound* (London, 1984), p.23.

132 Camfield, *Francis Picabia*, p.180.

133 Stock, p.311.

134 *Ibid.*, p.312.

135 *Ibid.*, pp.312–13; Lindberg-Seyersted, p.68; Morrill Cody, 'Ezra Pound, en Montparnasse', *L'Herne*, 6 (1965), p.145; Margaret Anderson, *My Thirty Years War* (London, 1930), p.252.

136 Clearfield, p.123.

137 Hamilton, pp.160–1.

138 Zinnes, p.172.

139 Christopher Green, *Léger and the Avant-Garde* (London, 1976), p.277.

140 Zinnes, p.172.

141 Clearfield, p.123.

142 Fernand Léger, 'The Esthetics of the Machine, Manufactured Objects, Artisan and Artist,' *The Little Review* (Spring, 1923), pp.45–9, and *ibid.* (Autumn–Winter, 1923–4), pp.55–8. The lecture was delivered on 1 June 1923, see Green, p.240. It was published in *Der Querschnitt*, 3 (1923), and in *Bulletin de l'Effort Moderne*, 1 (January 1924), and 2 (February 1924). The *Little Review* text is somewhat fuller than that of 1924 – of which an English translation is available in the Tate Gallery catalogue, *Léger and Purist Paris* (London 1970), pp.87–92.

143 *The Little Review* (Spring, 1923), p.45.

144 *Ibid.*, p.46.

145 *Ibid.* The final sentence is not in the 1924 text. Although in 1913 Picabia had invoked the Platonic proposition that beauty resides in geometrical and manufactured objects, his own art was soon to turn in the satirical direction we have seen, see Reyner Banham, *Theory and Design in the First Machine Age* (London, 1960), p.205. It may be worth comparing Léger's focus upon the humble utensils of the kitchen with the consolation Pound derives in *The Pisan Cantos* from the meanest objects – like his table – and forms of life.

146 *Gaudier*, p.26.

147 *Ibid.*, p.116.

148 *The Little Review* (Autumn–Winter, 1923–4), p.57. Not in the 1924 text.

149 *Ibid.*

150 *Ibid.*, p.55. Not in the 1924 text.

151 *Ezra Pound and Music*, ed. R. Murray Schafer (London, 1978), p.260.

152 Stock, pp.335, 337–8; Zinnes, pp.299–303; 'Machines, Introductory Letter', *The New Review* (Winter, 1931–2) (Zinnes, pp.215–17); see also n.199 below for George Antheil and Pound's thoughts on machines. On the limitations of photographs of sculpture, see Zinnes, pp.171–2, and *Literary Essays*, p.443.

153 Zinnes, pp.301–2.

154 *The Little Review* (Autumn–Winter, 1923–4), p.55.

155 *Bulletin de l'Effort Moderne*, 2 (February 1924), p.10: 'Les hommes de la Renaissance ont cru être supérieurs aux Primitifs, leur prédecesseurs, en imitant les formes naturelles au lieu d'en chercher l'équivalence . . .'

156 *Translations*, p.23.

157 *Ibid.*

158 Schafer, p.468; see also p.270.

159 The sense that there is an immanent order in the world, always dimly – or brightly – coming to consciousness, is crucial to *The Cantos*.

160 *Blast* 1, p.154; Schafer, p.261.

161 Review of Jean Cocteau, *Poésies, 1917–20*, *The Dial* (January 1921), p.110.

162 Green, p.275.

163 *Ibid.*, p.166.

164 *Ibid.*

165 *Ibid.*, pp.164–5, 181–2.

166 *Ibid.*

167 Davie, *Ezra Pound, Poet as Sculptor*, pp.123, 132–3.

168 Serge Fauchereau, *La Révolution Cubiste* (Paris, 1982), pp.179–83.

169 *The Dial* (January 1921), p.124; *Literary Review*, New York *Evening Post*, 13 August 1921, p.7.

170 Green, p.166.

171 *Ibid.*, pp.275–6; Judi Freeman, 'Léger re-examined', *Art History* (March 1984), pp.352–3.

172 Fernand Léger, *Functions of Painting*, ed. Edward F. Fry (London, 1973), pp.20–3.

173 *The Dial* (March 1923) (Zinnes, pp.175–7).

174 Green, pp.276–81.
175 *Ibid.*, p.279.
176 *Ibid.*
177 *Ibid.*
178 *Ibid.*, p.281.
179 Standish D. Lawder, *The Cubist Cinema* (New York, 1975), p.101ff.
180 *Ibid.*, p.114.
181 *Ibid.*, p.115.
182 Schafer, pp.481–2.
183 Lawder, pp.115–17, and n.60.
184 *Ibid.*, p.117.
185 Stock, p.253.
186 Freeman, p.353. Man Ray was also involved in shooting the film. For his account, see Lawder, p.118.
187 *Ibid.*, n.31.
188 *Ibid.*, p.353.
189 Fernand Léger, 'Mechanical Ballet', *The Little Review* (Autumn–Winter, 1924–5), pp.42–4.
190 Green, p.282.
191 *Ibid.*
192 Lawder, p.137.
193 Schafer, p.311.
194 *Antheil and the Treatise on Harmony* (Schafer, p.261).
195 *Ibid.*
196 *Ibid.* (Schafer, p.297).
197 *The New Age*, 25 November 1920 (Schafer, p.472). *ABC of Reading* (London, 1961), p.198 (Schafer, p.472).
198 *Antheil and the Treatise on Harmony* (Schafer, p.260).
199 'Antheil, 1924–1926', *New Criterion* (October 1926) (Schafer, p.315; see *ibid.*, pp.474–5).
200 Green, p.284.
201 Zinnes, pp.172–3.
202 Green, p.293.
203 *Ibid.*, p.295.
204 *Ibid.*, p.240.
205 Green, p.295.
206 *Ibid.*
207 *Ibid.*, p.295ff.
208 *Cantos*, p.590.
209 'Brancusi', p.445.
210 *Patria Mia*, quoted at Davie, *Ezra Pound* (Chicago, 1982), p.24.
211 'Antheil, 1924–1926', *New Criterion* (October 1926) (Schafer, p.315). 'Workshop Orchestration', *New Masses* (March 1927) (Schafer, pp.317–18).
212 'Ruskin was well-meaning but a goose. The remedy for machines is not pastoral retrogression. The remedy for the locomotive belching soft-coal smoke is not the stage-coach, but the electric locomotive . . .', 'The City', *The Exile* (Autumn 1928), *Selected Prose*, pp.194–5. At the Lyceum Club in March 1912 Marinetti spoke of 'your deplorable Ruskin . . . With his sick dream of a primitive pastoral life . . . with his hatred of the machine, of steam and electricity . . .' (Banham, p.123).
213 'Arnold Dolmetsch', *Literary Essays*, p.436 (Schafer, p.40).
214 Clearfield, p.130.
215 Stock, p.324.

Ezra Pound and Italian Art

PETER ROBINSON

Ezra Pound returned to Italy, and, of the four countries in which he lived, it was here that he longest made his home. He found inspiration in the landscape, in some of the cities' histories, in Italian music, poetry and art. Italy provided him with occasions and milieux; it also influenced his thinking about the ideal conditions for making art and for patronage. Pound's debts to the Pre-Raphaelites, Ruskin and Pater are reflected in allegiances to Romanesque and early Renaissance architecture, Quattrocento painting and sculpture. There are conflicts between the aesthetic and moral significances of craftsmen and artists, as of pagan and Christian images in the art he loved. Yet Pound's tastes have recurrent characteristics and values, while the manner in which he held, exemplified and expressed his tastes has important implications. He believed that a decadence occurred in Italian art about 1500, and explained this by the growing tolerance of usury. His various analogies associate the best in Quattrocento Italian art with his idealisation of Benito Mussolini as a potential economic reformer. With the collapse of these hopes in 1945, Pound, imprisoned outside Pisa, returned to his preferences in Italian art – cherishing values in the works he loved, but also reaffirming faith in his idea of Mussolini. My essay explores Ezra Pound's ideas and analogies to understand his attempt at an ordered vision of artistic and social values. I criticise some of his methods and separate out his associations to examine dangers in forced or assumed coherences; but his tastes in art may not be entirely dissociated from political and economic allegiances, for this would be to aestheticise his damagingly flawed, yet far more ambitious, life's work.

I Milieux and Patronage

In *Gaudier-Brzeska: a Memoir*, Ezra Pound recalls a moment when, sitting for his bust, he felt as if he were living in a renaissance:

> At any rate, there was I on a shilling wooden chair in a not over-heated studio with the railroad trains rushing overhead, and there was the half-ton block of marble on its stand, and bobbing about it was this head 'out of the renaissance.'[1]

He then casually notes a habit of mind that is at the heart of his poetic inspiration: 'I have now and again had the lark of escaping the present, and this was one of those expeditions.' Pound is careful to discriminate between a sense that he had merely seen the sculptor's face before in a work of art, and 'the veritable spirit of awakening'. He concludes:

> I knew that if I had lived in the Quattrocento I should have had no finer moment, and no better craftsman to fill it. And it is not a common thing to know that one is drinking the cream of the ages.

Significant here for a view of Ezra Pound's attachment to Italian art is his association of Gaudier's social position with that of the artist, as he saw it, in the early Renaissance. His 'not over-heated studio' coolly points to the young sculptor's difficulties in finding satisfactory conditions for work. Thus Pound found himself in a milieu which could set him 'thinking of renaissance life, of Leonardo, of Gonzaga, or Valla's praise of Nicolas V'; which is to say, thinking about artists, patrons and, perhaps, the relations between them.

Here I will be looking at Pound's interest in artists and patrons of the early Renaissance, and how it influenced his thoughts about where to live, and about the problem of financial support for the arts in our century. Hoping for a new 'spirit of awakening', he worked to ameliorate the then contemporary situation[2] yet saw that contemporaneity in the partial light of an historical analogy. Wyndham Lewis's astutely unsettling remarks on Pound in *Time and Western Man* are designed to alert us to the danger in his penchant for seeing himself and his contemporaries through precedents in history:

> He has really walked with Sophocles beside the Aegean; he has *seen* the Florence of Cavalcanti; there is almost nowhere in the Past that he has not visited . . . But where the present is concerned it is a different matter. He is extremely untrustworthy where that is concerned.[3]

Pound's description of Gaudier-Brzeska at work serves two purposes: it ennobles him by association with an exalted past moment; it criticises the present by pointing to the discrepancy between Gaudier's value, 'the veritable spirit of awakening', and his circumstances, 'a shilling wooden chair'.

Much of Pound's interest in the social position of the Quattrocento artist can be traced back to the brief career of penury and early death at the Front of his friend Gaudier-Brzeska. His means of understanding that waste, however, display a debt to Yeats's involvement in the loss of the Hugh Lane bequest, and poems related to it in *Responsibilities*, a volume Pound reviewed in *Poetry*, May 1914. Hugh Lane had insisted that his collection of modern French pictures be housed in a new gallery built on a 'bridge site across the Liffey to the design of Sir Edward Lutyens',[4] but there was concerted opposition to the plan and during the winter of 1912–13, Yeats became involved in the controversy. The outcome was, as Joseph Hone relates, that 'Lane carried the pictures away and lent them to the National Gallery in London, and Yeats enlarged the already rich body of his work by a number of fine political poems'. One of these pieces, 'To a Wealthy Man who Promised a Second Subscription to the Dublin Municipal Gallery if it were Proved the People Wanted Pictures', scolds the rich man by comparing him unfavourably with examples of Italian Renaissance patrons devoted to the encouragement of culture. Adopting a lofty disdain for 'the blind and ignorant town', Yeats's poem gives three instances to emphasise the individual ruler and patron who instigates the work; each turns on an indifference to popular opinion; and each is set in an Italian city-state. The second is the most succinct:

> And Guidobaldo, when he made
> That grammar school of courtesies
> Where wit and beauty learned their trade
> Upon Urbino's windy hill,
> Had sent no runners to and fro
> That he might learn the shepherds' will.[5]

Ezra Pound does not refer to the poem in his review, 'The Later Yeats'; but his remarking that 'one has felt his work becoming gaunter, seeking greater hardness of outline'[6] would apply to this poem – where the 'hardness' may be felt both in the plain diction and the direct tone with which the poem's indirect rebuke is brought home.

'Villanelle: the Psychological Hour' (1915), one of Pound's best shorter poems, yet uncharacteristically faltering and diffident, has long been thought to refer to Sophie and Henri Gaudier-Brzeska – 'No word from her nor him' – largely on the strength of a passage from Pound's memoir which seems also to voice the charged disappointment and self-doubt present in the poem's tentative autobiographical note. Pound writes, in the Gaudier memoir, how he 'knew that many things would bore or disgust him, particularly my rather middle-aged point of view, my intellectual tiredness and exhaustion, my general scepticism and quietness . . .'[7] This is not exactly self-knowledge, rather the sketch for a persona that culminates in *Hugh Selwyn Mauberley* (1920); but, more immediately, it produced:

> Now the third day is here –
>   no word from either;
> No word from her nor him,
> Only another man's note:
>   'Dear Pound, I am leaving England.'[8]

'"*Between the night and morning?*"', one of the poem's most tantalising lines, comes
from W. B. Yeats's 'The People':

> The daily spite of this unmannerly town,
> Where who has served the most is most defamed,
> The reputation of his lifetime lost
> Between the night and morning.[9]

This poem also alludes to Renaissance life, and, evidently another piece written
out of rebarbative discouragement, continues:

> I might have lived,
> And you know well how great the longing has been,
> Where every day my footfall should have lit
> In the green shadow of Ferrara wall . . .[10]

Yeats's poem, like Pound's 'Villanelle', is concerned with choice of milieu, and the
artist's right to choose –

> I might have used the one substantial right
> My trade allows: chosen my company,
> And chosen what scenery had pleased me best.[11]

The 'might have' tense defines an impossibility in Yeats's lines, where Pound's
much more laconic, hesitant treatment leaves a choice open. We can, however,
hear the Yeatsian aristocratic note in Pound's essay of 1914, 'The Renaissance',
when he writes that 'scholars of the quattrocento . . . did not give the crowd what it
wanted.'[12] There too he reflects upon the relation between modern capital cities
and Renaissance city-states as cultural centres. The revival of classical learning
and the study of Roman antiquities did not result in 'a single great vortex' (and by
using that word Pound associates Rome with Vorticist London), 'but it did result in
the numerous vortices of the Italian cities, striving against each other not only in
commerce but in the arts as well.'[13] The foundations for Ezra Pound's hero-
worship of Sigismondo Malatesta as art patron are being laid here.

What was Pound looking for in Italy? *The Cantos* contains descriptions of
landscapes and places which are principally and recurrently Italian. Unlike W. B.
Yeats, when Pound calls forth a past moment he shortens the perspective of loss
and attempts to re-establish poetically a state of mind as if from within that
moment. In 1915 he began composing a long poem he had begun contemplating
as early as 1911.[14] 'Three Cantos' were published in *Poetry* during 1917, revised
and collected in *Quia Pauper Amavi* (1919). By the end of 1920 Pound had written
seven cantos, but was growing dissatisfied with their shape. In May 1922 he
published a Canto VIII in *The Dial* which subsequently became Canto II in *A Draft*

of XVI Cantos (1925); there, the third of 'Three Cantos' was revised into Canto I and the first was radically condensed into Canto III.[15] His evocations of Italian scenery in 'Three Cantos' are populated with visionary traces of gods and goddesses. For Pound, the desire to experience the presence of pagan deities is bound up with sensations of Italian scenery. Moreover, these favoured landscapes, described in an incantatory manner which creates a rêverie-like state in the reader, are occasionally interspersed with allusions to Italian artists.[16] The present Canto III begins this thread by locating the poet in Venice in 1908, 'I sat on the Dogana's steps'; within this opening section we hear:

> . . . the leaves are full of voices,
> A-whisper, and the clouds bowe over the lake,
> And there are gods upon them,
> And in the water, the almond-white swimmers,
> The silvery water glazes the upturned nipple,
> As Poggio has remarked.[17]

There are of course no lakes in Venice. The passage is a condensation from the 'Three Cantos' of 1917; there the Venetian setting and the vision of Lake Garda are clearly, but distractingly, differentiated. In April 1910 Dorothy and Olivia Shakespear joined Ezra Pound at Sirmione; their visit 'influenced both Dorothy and Ezra profoundly'.[18] The rejected 'First Canto' is a garrulous monologue by Pound addressed to Robert Browning; the addressee survives in only the first three lines of the present Canto II, but in the old first canto it is precariously sustained throughout.

Though the addressee is consistent as nowhere in *The Cantos*, the location is not; and in this it prefigures Pound's method until history intervened to give *The Pisan Cantos* a recurrently present single location. Ezra Pound's technical problem in the first of 'Three Cantos' is that while he remains residually attached to the principle of a poem's location in one place and to a continuous speaking voice, he also wants thematically to juxtapose extremely diverse material located in different landscapes and scenes:

> Sirmio serves my will better than your Asolo
> Which I have never seen.
>   Your 'palace step'?
> My stone seat was the Dogana's curb . . .[19]

It is not merely a technical problem, for the repeated questions put to Browning dramatise over-consciously, and, indeed, exemplify, a lack of confidence in the thematic endeavour – which at this stage, might be described as an effort to restore immediate experience of the pagan world. To achieve this, Pound needed a

[125]

suitable milieu, and the first of 'Three Cantos' has him speculating on whether his experiences of Italy (which he is remembering from England in wartime) are in fact sufficient. 'True, it was Venice,' he notes, and 'So, for what it's worth, I have the background.'[20]

When he returns to Sirmio, the haunt of Catullus on Lake Garda, 'The background' becomes a world. However, unlike the equivalent passage which opens the revised Canto III, the old version's interjectory style implicitly doubts the presence of the gods which the lines rescued from it take for granted. 'Gods float in the azure air,/ Bright gods, and Tuscan, back before dew was shed' was originally followed by 'Is it a world like Puvis?'[21] But the French symbolist painter Puvis de Chavannes, and his pastel-coloured visions, are immediately rejected: 'Never so pale, my friend . . .' To present the gods like this in his poem is nevertheless to imply that he himself isn't quite sure what they would look like. Further revisions serve to assume the gods' presence:

> . . . Our olive Sirmio
> Lies in its burnished mirror, and the Mounts of Balde and Riva
> Are alive with song, and all the leaves are full of voices.
> '*Non è fuggito.*'
>   'It is not gone.' Metastasio
> Is right – we have that world about us,
> And the clouds bow above the lake, and there are folk upon them[22]

In the revised version, there are 'gods' on the clouds instead of 'folk'. Towards the end of this false start, Pound seems to admit that he is concocting a fantasy, rather than presenting an experience: 'No, take it all for lies'; but then in the upward curve of the canto's close he invokes Botticelli's 'The Birth of Venus' and the 'Primavera' to buoy up the failing confidence in his access to the pagan spirit world. He wonders whether he shall

>   . . . confuse the thing I see
> With actual gods behind me?
>   Are they gods behind me?
> How many worlds we have! If Botticelli
> Brings her ashore on that great cockle-shell –
> His Venus (Simonetta?),
> And Spring and Aufidus fill all the air
> With their clear-outlined blossoms?
> World enough. Behold, I say, she comes . . .[23]

'Behold, I say' gives the lie to this passage, though; for to call us to see ('Behold') is one thing, to ask us to take the poet's word for it ('I say') another. Ezra Pound was right to cut these lines, but what this means is that he was right to replace a passage which is in two minds about whether the visionary world of Renaissance paganism is accessible to him, with lines whose propositional directness we are to take as literally true: 'And there are gods upon them'. For all its stale Browningese, the first of 'Three Cantos' is recognisably in the sceptical present, and no more so than when Pound turns to Quattrocento painting as a means of visualising the deities. We too can see these works of art, and finding goddesses returned through real woods is an experience of a different order to that of seeing them in pictures.

In his essay 'Cavalcanti' (1910–31), Pound says that 'We appear to have lost the radiant world where one thought cuts through another with clean edge',[24] for example, 'the glass under water, the form that seems a form seen in a mirror'. This world which is untouched by 'St Clement of Alexandria, with his prohibition of bathing by women' sponsors that beautiful line 'The silvery water glazes the upturned nipple'.[25] Pound saw in Quattrocento art a world of women without Christian shame, and *The Cantos* are, in part, endeavouring to discover and present the conditions for such an art in such a world.

His rejected first canto comes to a close with further allusions to painters. Where earlier the question of a suitable milieu had been approached as a matter of 'background' and then 'world', here 'worlds' seem equivalents of 'brave *décors*' – a word hinting at a connection between fresco design or Vorticist interior decoration, and that world of crystalline forms:

> Mantegna a sterner line, and the new world about us:
> Barred lights, great flares, new form, Picasso or Lewis.
> If for a year man write to paint, and not to music —[26]

This is the version printed in *Poetry* (Chicago); the *Quia Pauper Amavi* text dropped the association of Mantegna's line with Cubist or Vorticist painting. The particular Mantegnas that Pound had in mind are made evident in the opening of the second of 'Three Cantos', and here I quote the much improved *Quia Pauper Amavi* version:

> Send out your thought upon the Mantuan palace,
> Drear waste, great halls; pigment flakes from the stone;
> Forlorner quarter;
> Silk tatters still in the frame, Gonzaga's splendour,
> Where do we come upon the ancient people . . .[27]

Andrea Mantegna (c.1431–1506) painted frescoes in the *Camera degli Sposi* (Bridal Chamber) at the Palazzo Ducale in Mantua during 1473–4; they are a glorification of the ruling Gonzaga family. Pound's allusion to Mantegna's decorations survives in Canto III as an image for cultural decline:

> Drear waste, the pigment flakes from the stone,

> Or plaster flakes, Mantegna painted the wall.
> Silk tatters, 'Nec Spe Nec Metu.'[28]

Daniel Pearlman observes:

> The decay of the Renaissance is most powerfully suggested in the final line of
> the canto . . . in which the stoic motto of the Este family, 'With neither hope
> nor fear,' is contrasted with the decay that supervened when the Estes fell
> away from this noble precept.[29]

The Estes were the ruling house of Ferrara; Isabella d'Este was married to
Francesco Gonzaga, and had her family motto embroidered on tapestry in the
Ducal Palace in Mantua. She figures in the history of relations between patrons
and artists through the survival of correspondence attempting to commission
works for her Grotta decorated in accordance with her taste for 'allegorical fantasy
based upon pagan myth'.[30]

D. S. Chambers in *Patrons and Artists in the Italian Renaissance* describes her as
'sharp-witted and cultivated rather than learned' but concludes: 'Not only was
Isabella d'Este fastidious and importunate . . . she was not over generous in
payment, so that one may suspect that her princely patronage was hardly
something an established painter would go out of his way to seek.'[31] Pound was
also aware of Isabella d'Este's shortcomings as a patron, and the appearance of
her motto in tatters at the end of Canto III may be designed to represent both
the decay of the Gonzagas and one indication of why it happened. In a letter of
31 March 1925 to Henry Allen Moe, secretary to the John Simon Guggenheim
Memorial Foundation, Pound wrote:

> The good artist goes on seeing flaws in his work long after the bad artist is
> glad to have it finished and palm it off onto someone less easy to please.
>   You can find this in the record of relations between a society woman like
> Isabella D'Este and Mantegna or Perugino. It is possibly not mere coincidence
> that Leonardo da Vinci went up to Fiesole when Isabella came to Florence.[32]

Yet one of the Gonzagas figures in *The Cantos* as a representative of exceptionally
enlightened patronage, second only to Sigismondo Malatesta. Ludovico Gonzaga
lured Mantegna from Padua in 1459 by offering him the generous salary of 15
ducats a month as well as accommodation and living expenses. Mantegna was to
complain about the irregularity of his payment, but, as Vasari noted:

> Genius is not always recognized and rewarded as it was in the case of Andrea
> Mantegna, an artist who was born of very humble stock in the Mantua
> district, working in the fields as a boy and yet . . . rising to the rank of a knight
> through his own efforts and good fortune.[33]

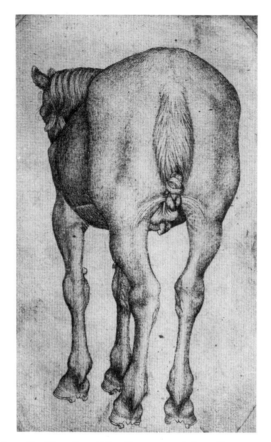

Pisanello, 'Horse from Behind', 1433–8? *Codex Vallardi, Louvre*

Vasari also comments that Ludovico 'always valued and patronized Andrea's talents', which is indicated both by the salary he offered and his concern that Mantegna should finish the altarpiece in San Zeno, Verona, to his satisfaction before moving to Mantua: 'if these six months are not enough for you,' he writes, 'take seven or eight, so that you can finish everything you have begun and come here with your mind at rest.'[34] Recognition of the artist's status, concern for his state of mind and his financial security are all in marked contrast to the situation of Gaudier-Brzeska: a polemical contrast is implicit in Pound's citing the Gonzagas when imagining Gaudier's head '"out of the renaissance."'

Michael Baxandall observes that Mantegna 'in return for his salary not only painted frescoes and panels for the Gonzagas, but filled other functions as well.'[35] Ezra Pound liked this sense of the artist's integrating into different aspects of court

[129]

Pisanello, obverse of 'Portrait of Gianfrancesco I Gonzaga', 1439-44
The Syndics of the Fitzwilliam Museum

life and his wide usefulness to the patron. In the *ABC of Reading* he contrasts himself with Pisanello (*c.*1395 –*c.*1455):

> No one would be foolish enough to send me to pick out a horse or even an automobile for him.
> Pisanello painted horses so that one remembers the painting, and the Duke of Milan sent him to Bologna to BUY horses.[36]

Pisanello's letter concerning the matter is translated in Canto XXVI. Michael Baxandall, however, emphasises the exceptional nature of Ludovico Gonzaga's patronage: 'But Mantegna's position was unusual among the great Quattrocento painters; even those who produced paintings for princes were more commonly paid for a piece of work than as permanent salaried retainers.'[37] The Ferrarese painter Francesco del Cossa (*c.*1435 –*c.*1478) worked under much less exalted conditions. Borso d'Este, celebrated in the Schifanoia Frescoes at Ferrara and in *The Cantos*, paid for work on those frescoes at the rate of ten Bolognese *lire* for the square *pede*. Del Cossa wrote complaining about this method of payment at a fixed rate for the area covered.[38]

In this light, the letter Sigismondo Malatesta wrote to Giovanni de' Medici on 7 April 1449 about attracting a painter from Florence to Rimini seems extra-

Pisanello, 'Portrait of Sigismondo Malatesta', 1445
The Syndics of the Fitzwilliam Museum

ordinarily generous, combining elements particularly attractive to a twentieth-century artist like Pound. Sigismondo Malatesta (1417–68) ruled in Rimini from 1432 until his death. He is chiefly remembered for the Tempio Malatestiano, a Christian church dedicated to San Francesco. In 1447 he began remodelling the 'original thirteenth-century Gothic church into a "temple of fame" celebrating, among other things, his love for his mistress (later his third wife) Isotta degli Atti . . .'[39] Sigismondo's letter to Giovanni de' Medici constitutes the first main section of the first of the four Malatesta Cantos; thus it concentrates our attention on Malatesta as art patron, and, following on the previous canto's diagnosis of inertia and lethargy in English culture, contrasts with 'The house too thick, the paintings / a shade too oiled'.[40] Canto VIII indicates that a '*Maestro di pentore*' has been found to paint the chapels in the Tempio, but

> That there can be no question of
> His painting the walls for the moment,
> As the mortar is not yet dry. . .[41]

However, Sigismondo writes proposing to take the painter into his service, offering, like Ludovico Gonzaga, 'so much per year'; he will 'arrange for him to paint something else'[42] until the chapels are ready, and he closes the letter

[131]

Matteo de' Pasti, 'Portrait of Isotta degli Atti', 1446
The Syndics of the Fitzwilliam Museum

reaffirming his intention to provide the artist with security.

> For I mean to give him good treatment
> So that he may come to live the rest
> Of his life in my lands –
> Unless you put him off it –
> And for this I mean to make due provision,
> So that he can work as he likes,
> Or waste his time as he likes. . .[43]

The last two lines particularly appealed to Pound. He quotes them in the original here, and, emphasising an affinity he sees between Malatesta and Thomas Jefferson as patrons, repeats '*affatigandose per suo piacer o non*' in Canto XXI[44] after a letter of Jefferson's about hiring domestic servants who would double as musicians in a chamber orchestra. What I imagine particularly attracted Ezra Pound to the terms of Sigismondo's letter is that it combines freedom from material anxieties with freedom to exercise his talent as he desires.

Leon Battista Alberti (1404–72) was Sigismondo's architect for the Tempio. In his book on this pioneer of Renaissance neo-classicism, Franco Borsi indicates that the master of painting alluded to in Sigismondo's letter was either Filippo Lippi or

Matteo de' Pasti, obverse of 'Portrait of Isotta degli Atti', 1446
The Syndics of the Fitzwilliam Museum

Gentile da Fabriano.[45] Though Piero della Francesca (c.1410–92) painted 'Sigismondo Malatesta kneeling before St Sigismund' (1451) in the sacristy of the Tempio, the chapels were never frescoed, but decorated with bas-reliefs, and it must be assumed that the arrangements proposed in the Canto VIII letter came to nothing. Sigismondo did however manage to attract artists and, as Pound notes in the *Guide to Kulchur*, he does seem to have 'had a little of the best there in Rimini'.[46] Why Pound particularly admired the princes of city-states as art patrons, especially when they made their artists salaried retainers, is that they thus produced milieux for the artists' mutual support; Pound seems to have thrived on the intellectual exchanges of such a milieu in his best London years. He wrote in a letter:

> From the patron's angle, Giusto de Conti and Bassinio were the best poets of their day . . . they stretched their legs under the same table that had received Pier della Francesca, Pisanello, Giovan Bellini, Battista Alberti, Mino da Fiesole; and the young Bassinio, at least, profited, presumably in head as well as in stomach.[47]

This attachment to the ideal of an artistic community also influences the kind of Italian art that Pound singled out for praise. In Canto XLV he criticises, as among the evil effects of usury.[48] the decline of fresco in favour of easel painting. The Mantegnas in the *Camera degli Sposi* at Mantua (colour plate, p.29) figure once more:

> with usura
> seeth no man Gonzaga his heirs and his concubines
> no picture is made to endure nor to live with
> but it is made to sell and sell quickly . . .[49]

Easel paintings are made in studios and then transported to the client so the patron need no longer make the artist a home; and, worse, the framed painting on a panel or piece of canvas can be readily resold. In his 'Paris Letter' which appeared in *The Dial* of January 1923, Pound, while elegising 'that painting ought to be part of architecture; that there is no place for sculpture or painting in modern life', observed:

> The stuff is vendible or non-vendible, it is scraps, knick-knacks, part of the disease that gives us museums instead of temples, curiosity shops instead of such rooms as the hall of the Palazzo Pubblico in Siena or of the Sala di Notari in Perugia.[50]

A curious analogy of the economic relations inherent in fresco painting as contrasted with canvas or panel appears in Canto XLV; Pound implies a distinction between 'whores for Eleusis'[51] and Gonzaga's 'concubines'. The latter, like frescoes, are to 'live with'; the former are sold like paintings, through single transactions with different clients. The canto thus displays a categorical objection to the negotiation of terms for individual works, and to the painter marketing his skills; but his evidence for enlightened anti-usurious economic relations between artist and patron may derive only from the exceptional instances of extremely generous, enlightened princes.

Canto XXV presents evidence for the decline of such ideal relations, in the form of documents about the dealings of Titian (*c.*1485–1576) with the Venetian Council. An initial fragment seems to indicate the painter complaining about both the location of the wall decorations he is to produce, and the terms of employment:

> . . . side toward the piazza, the worst side of the room
> that no one has been willing to tackle,
> and do it as cheap or much cheaper . . .[52]

D. S. Chambers gives the full letter, and, in his note, suggests that it is Titian's own eagerness to gain the commission which explains the apparently humiliating terms of employment. Missing from Pound's canto is any indication of rivalry between Titian and the aged Giovanni Bellini (*c.*1430–1516) that Chambers finds in the surviving documents. Pound's translation also implicitly exaggerates the degree of humiliation in the terms. Chambers reads: 'I shall begin, if it pleases Your Sublimity, with the canvas of the Battle scene on the side towards the Piazza, which is the most difficult, and nobody yet has wanted to attempt such a task.'[53] This suggests that the painting is difficult, not the wall. Titian writes that he will 'accept for my work any payment that might be thought convenient, or much less' because he is asking for 'the first *sansaria* for life that shall be vacant in the *Fondaco dei Tedeschi*'. This letter is dated 31 May 1513 and is followed in Canto xxv by a document from the Council dated 11 August 1522 moving that Titian 'be constrained to finish said canvas'[54] and then threatening to relieve him of the 'brokerage on the Fondamenta delli Thodeschi' which he had been granted in return for the mural work. Finally, in 1537, the Council had grown tired of waiting for Titian to finish the work and voted that:

> Tician de Cadore, pictor, be by authority of this Council
> obliged and constrained to restore to our government all the
> moneys that he has had from the agency during the time he
> has not worked on the painting in the said
> hall as is reasonable . . .[55]

Pound's interpretation of the original document makes the Venetian Council appear to be exploiting and then victimising Titian; in the light of Chambers's translation the culpabilities seem more evenly divided. Wethey, in *The Painting of Titian*, tells us that the work was repeatedly put off because 'The artist's fame had spread abroad, and requests for his services came from the great princes of Italy, as well as from Emperor Charles v.'[56] He also interprets the document with which Pound concludes Canto xxv by noting that the Council 'threatened to demand the reimbursement of all moneys given hitherto to him'; nor does Pound point out that Titian then completed the mural and was not obliged to repay the sums.

Further instances of decline are offered in the next canto when Vittore Carpaccio (c.1450–c.1525/6) writes to Francesco Gonzaga, Isabella d'Este's husband, about a 'Jerusalem' which Gonzaga's painter Lorenzo had seen and wanted to purchase, presumably for Mantua: 'Finally the deal was made and he took it away, without paying and hasn't since then appeared.'[57] Thus in Canto xxvi, Carpaccio is writing to Gonzaga asking to be paid for a work which has been removed from his studio. If Pound's translation is compared with Chambers's version and the original, there are further problems of interpretation, and interpolation. Chambers reads: 'Since the deal was concluded and his good faith pledged, he has never appeared again.'[58] The original states: 'Finalment concluso il mercato cum il dar de la fede mai più è comparso'[59] – which lacks Pound's 'and he took it away, without paying'. Later in the letter, Pound writes that 'this painter of yours has carried off a piece, not the whole of it' and Chambers: 'It is certainly very true that our painter has carried off an entire section of this work done on a smaller scale, which I sold as it is . . .' and the original: 'Ben è vero che so certissimamente il prefato pictor vostro ne ha portato uno pezzo non integro et in forma picola il qual ho veduto come il sta.' Chambers has 'our painter' for 'vostro' which must be a slip of translation or proof-reading. It appears, though, that Carpaccio has sold a small version of part of the 'Jerusalem' to Francesco's painter. Both 'Views of Jerusalem' are among Carpaccio's lost works; a picture of that title, though whether the large or small version is not known, disappeared in the Sack of Mantua of 1630.

In his letter, Carpaccio suspects Lorenzo of wanting to plagiarise the large version; Carpaccio is trying to sell it directly to Mantua in the fear that the deal made with Francesco's painter was a ruse to look at the painting and copy it. This is bad enough, but it suggests that Carpaccio suspects bad faith principally on the part of a fellow painter; the letter involves professional rivalry in a competitive market. Pound seems to think that there is only one 'Jerusalem' and that Lorenzo has stolen part of it; this doesn't make sense in the light of his interpolation, and Pound seems either to have got the wrong end of the stick or to have consciously added to the letter so as to make the evidence for decline in standards of patronage more clear-cut. It serves better to introduce the very free version of a letter of Mozart's vigorously complaining about his predicament.[60] Ezra Pound wants to be able to read the particular, variously specific examples of economic relations as a moralised historical shape.

In the *ABC of Reading*, he makes a number of passing remarks which confirm that he felt a decline began in Italian painting at approximately the end of the Quattrocento. Of a 'Christ emerging from the tomb' by Perugino (*c.*1445–1523) he notes that such works 'of perfect ripeness often have nothing wrong in themselves, and yet serve as points from which we can measure a decadence'.[61] Canto XLV would lead one to think that this decay resulted from economic conditions such as those which appear in *The Cantos* to disadvantage Titian and Carpaccio. In 'Murder by Capital' (1933) Pound abandons the hope that individual contemporary patrons such as John Quinn, by then dead, could significantly improve the artist's situation: 'one intelligent millionaire *might* have done a good deal.' Instead, he pins his hopes on the reform of the economic system, and makes an association between the Quattrocento and the 1930s:

Mussolini is the first head of a state in our time to perceive and to proclaim *quality* as a dimension in national production. He is the first man in power to publish any such recognition *since*, since whom? – since Sigismond Malatesta . . .[62]

And why is Pound concerned with this 'fanciful kinship'[63] between Fascist leader and *condottiero* art patron? 'The unemployment problem that I have been faced with, for a quarter of a century . . . has been the problem of the unemployment of Gaudier-Brzeska, T. S. Eliot, Wyndham Lewis the painter, E. P. the present writer . . .'[64] The association of Gaudier with the Renaissance in Pound's memoir came to represent the failure of a usurious culture to recognise good art; further, that modern art's affinity with Quattrocento styles came to imply its resistance to the values of the society which had not properly recognised and employed it. Ezra Pound's moral simplification of the economic relations involved in Quattrocento art thus contributes distressingly to his idealisation of Benito Mussolini.

II Craftsmen and Artists

When Pound wrote of Gaudier-Brzeska at work, 'I knew that if I had lived in the Quattrocento I should have had no finer moment, and no better craftsman to fill it',[65] his phrase 'better craftsman' alludes to Dante's description of Arnaut Daniel as the 'miglior fabbro'[66] – the words T. S. Eliot later applied to Pound when dedicating *The Waste Land* to him. But was Gaudier like a Quattrocento artist or a twelfth-century craftsman? As early as *The Spirit of Romance* (1910), Pound had linked the troubadour poet with stone-carving: 'The Twelfth Century, or, more exactly, that century whose center is the year 1200, has left us two perfect gifts: the church of San Zeno in Verona, and the canzoni of Arnaut Daniel . . .'[67] Pound was in Verona in 1910, and Noel Stock suggests that 'In correcting the proofs of *The Spirit of Romance* he may have added (or strengthened) the remarks on San Zeno'.[68] A detail of its interior came to be emblematic of that perfection: the column signed by its maker in the crypt.

He returned to the significance of San Zeno in a 'Paris Letter' of December 1922, describing a visit to the church in July 1911 when William Carlos Williams's brother Edgar, an architect,

> came on Adamo San Guglielmo's signed column. Adamo was the architect, and is said to have cut some or most of the stone himself. Williams looked at the two simple spirals of red marble cut in one block, and burst out, 'How the hell do you expect us to get any buildings when we have to order our columns by the gross?'[69]

That Ezra Pound believed Adamo to have been the architect as well as the stone-carver explains why, in Canto XLV, it is not the column which is signed but the building: 'Came no church of cut stone signed: *Adamo me fecit*.'[70] The Edgar Williams anecdote is retold in Cantos LXXVIII and XCI. What seems important to

Pound is the practice of hand-carving which unites the sculptured detail on the church with the structural elements, the carved blocks and columns. As Pound goes on to note in the 'Paris Letter': 'A real building is one on which the eye can light and stay lit. The detail must bear inspection.'[71] It is a principle derived from John Ruskin that decoration and structure should be integrated, and that this integral relation will depend upon handmade stone-work.

Ruskin, too, admired San Zeno and the signed column. In the first volume of *The Stones of Venice*, he discusses twisted columns in relation to the natural forms of trees, and later notes of the San Zeno column:

> Its workman was proud of it, as well he might be: he has written his name upon its front (I would that more of his fellows had been as kindly vain), and the goodly stone proclaims forever, ADAMINUS DE SANCTO GIORGIO ME FECIT.[72]

Do Ruskin and Pound admire San Zeno for the same reason? Ruskin uses the same word of praise as Pound when commenting on the main door:

John Ruskin, 'The Signed Column', San Zeno, Verona
plate 17 from *The Stones of Venice*

how perfect in its simplicity the single entrance may become, when it is treated as in the Duomo and St Zeno of Verona . . . having noble porches, and rich sculptures grouped around the entrance.

Neither writer expects sculpture to have the perfection of machine-cut stone, and both employ the word to signify the best that men can do; but in 'The Nature of Gothic', Ruskin advances the influential distinction between machine work and handcraft: 'Men were not intended to work with the accuracy of tools, to be precise and perfect in all their actions.'[73] Here 'perfect' contains an ethical discrimination founded on Ruskin's Christian belief and the nature of man. Upon this Pound and Ruskin part company. When Ruskin writes of San Zeno as 'perfect in its simplicity', he has a contrast in mind with later architecture, and his word 'simplicity' also contains an ethical discrimination deriving from his faith.

Ruskin examines the decline of Venetian architecture by evaluating funereal sculpture. Of Tomaso Moncenigo's tomb he observes, 'its tabernacle above is still Gothic, and the recumbent figure is very beautiful. It was carved by two Florentine sculptors in 1423.'[74] Pound alludes to this doge and cites the date in Canto XXXV.[75] Moncenigo's successor Francesco Foscari died in 1457, and by this date the fall has occurred, for Ruskin detects 'the pride of state in its gradual intrusion upon the sepulchre' which ousts 'expressions of religious feeling and heavenly hope' in favour of 'arrogant setting forth of the virtues of the dead.'[76] Ruskin reinforces this sense of a decay in the work's spiritual meaning by finding craftsmanship whose criteria for success are derived from the viewpoint of men and not God's eye. Referring to sculpted figures on the Foscari tomb, he notes, 'Temperance, and Justice opposite to her, as neither the left hand of the one nor the right hand of the other could be seen from below, have been *left with one hand each*.'[77]

In his opening to *The Stones of Venice*, Ruskin refers to the 'undistinguished enchantment' of architecture which comes after this fall, where we may read 'in the brightness of their accumulated marble, pages on which the sentence of her luxury was to be written'. Pound too believes that there was a point of fall; in his essay 'Cavalcanti' he offers the date 1527.[78] He, like Ruskin, writes against luxury; in a contribution to *The New Age* for 12 February 1920, he describes the 'infamy' of the plumage trade as 'a by-product of the degradation of the sense of beauty into a sense of luxury';[79] and in Canto XXVI he presents the wife of a doge who 'would touch food but with forks' and explains 'with small golden prongs / Bringing in, thus, the vice of luxuria'.[80] For Ruskin the decline in architecture and rise of worldliness are attributable to the decay of a medieval Christian humility, and his later attacks on usury are supported by a belief about the innate sinfulness of men which must be actively resisted, as their potential goodness is actively fostered. Pound did not share such a belief in man's sinfulness, and his denunciations of usury consort with attacks on other people, particular individuals whose intentions are inexplicably corrupted.

Canto XLII presents the founding of the Sienese bank, the Monte dei Paschi, which was to '"keep bridle on usury"' (Canto XLIV);[81] in Canto XLII too Pound recalls San Zeno and Andrea Mantegna's altarpiece there whose predella panels show two cities on hilltops:

> so that the echo turned back in my mind: Pavia:
> Saw cities move in one figure, Vicenza, as depicted
> San Zeno by Adige . . .[82]

Canto XLV and the *Guide to Kulchur* confirm that San Zeno's style and craftsmanship came to stand for Pound as exemplary of a culture not financed by usury. Peter Faulkner in 'Pound and the Pre-Raphaelites' observes that 'the great denouncer of "Usura" makes no reference, so far as I know, to *The Stones of Venice* and all that followed from it'.[83] There are a few passing but significant references

Pietro Lombardo, Santa Maria dei Miracoli, Venice, 1480–9

to the volume and Ruskin's ideas in Pound's 'Art Notes' for *The New Age*. A piece
for 12 September 1918 called 'Buildings: Ornamentation!' observes:

> John Ruskin was the only man who ever worried over the horrors of 19th-
> century British architecture and John Ruskin was driven insane. Ruskin's
> fussy little copies of the Stones of Venice and Ruskin's final insanity should be
> perfectly understandable to anyone who spends even half an hour in
> observing the ornamentation of Oxford Street.[84]

In the same piece, written while Pound could not visit Italy because of the Great
War, he 'sighs for the stone window-frames of Verona'. Two reasons for his
distance from Ruskin are hinted at in this article. He rejects the Arts and Crafts
temptation to try putting the clock back: 'I am not sighing for the impossibilities of
fine carving, I do not expect people in our time to have a gross of Pietro Lombardos
sent down from Sheffield'; and he rejects the tendency to reproduce historical
styles in modern materials: 'The cement imitations of Pietro Lombardo's
mermaids set into brick façades are unspeakable abomination.'[85] Pietro Lombardo
(*c.*1435–1515) was also both architect and sculptor; he owes his fame to the
church of Santa Maria dei Miracoli in Venice, built between 1480 and 1489. The
carved mermaids are inside the church, and Pound repeatedly alludes to them as
instances of concord between the material and style of both architecture and
ornament.[86]

In 'Modern Manufacture and Design', Ruskin also criticises the attempt to
transfer aesthetic qualities achieved in one medium to another: 'No man who
knows what painting means, can endure a painted glass window which emulates
painters' work.'[87] He also states the connection Pound affirms between good
ornament and milieux: 'Portable art – independent of all place – is for the most
part ignoble art.'[88] Another of Pound's *New Age* articles, 'Super-fronts', indicates
the more fundamental divergence from Ruskin. He is speculating on why London
facade ornaments are so bad, and suggests 'the mania for completion' as a reason:

> The cathedrals were often a long while in building. One could at least leave
> the blocks in the rough until the talent arrived. The unfinished blocks would
> serve as an incentive to young sculptors. When one thinks of Gaudier-Brzeska
> too poor to buy stone for his work, one can readily believe that had the Ritz
> blocks been left rough, he would have been often only too glad to carve them
> at a guinea a mask; and Piccadilly would have been that much the richer.
>
> The Stones of Venice which gave such delight to John Ruskin must have
> been carved upon some such system.[89]

This is rather impractical-sounding, and 'carved upon some such system' implies

Pound's lack of interest in or knowledge of why Ruskin thought the sculptural ornament was so fine.

Crucial to Ruskin's theory is the usually anonymous, skilled, but necessarily imperfect craftsman who is motivated in his work by piety. His aesthetic distinction between machine-worked and hand-cut stone is founded upon a version of the *felix culpa*; he believes his faith to be the moving spirit within the architecture he admires. The Christian view of man's nature certainly informs the principles he adduces from it:

> Enough, I trust, has been said to show the reader that the rudeness or imperfection which at first rendered the term 'Gothic' one of reproach is indeed, when rightly understood, one of the most noble characters of Christian architecture, and not only a noble but an *essential* one.[90]

The problem with Pound's word 'perfect' as applied to San Zeno lies in the incompatibility of aesthetic perfection with the Christian view of human nature. Pound would have to explain its qualities in terms of the economic structure alone. The craftsman's Christian humility in the process of working his stone is not emphasised. This divergence of principle on the significance of architecture such as San Zeno in Verona extends to the implications of the signed column for each of them.

When Ruskin allows the workman to be 'proud of it, as well he might be' he also registers a moral qualm about the possible sins of pride or vanity in this lack of

Pietro Lombardo, Mermaids, Santa Maria dei Miracoli, Venice

[142]

anonymity; in 'I would that more of his fellows had been as kindly vain', 'kindly' is pressed to deflect the charge in 'vain' by suggesting both generous and natural impulses. The contextual nuances of Canto XLV are quite different:

> . . . Pietro Lombardo
> came not by usura
> Duccio came not by usura
> nor Pier della Francesca; Zuan Bellin' not by usura
> nor was 'La Calunnia' painted.
> Came not by usura Angelico; came not Ambrogio Praedis,
> Came no church of cut stone signed: *Adamo me fecit*.[91]

The 'Duccio' of this passage is not Duccio di Buoninsegna, the Sienese painter, but Agostino di Duccio (1413–81) who carved many of the bas-reliefs in Sigismondo Malatesta's Tempio between 1449 and 1457. Giovanni Bellini was most admired by Pound for his 'Cristo Morto Sorretto da Quattro Angeli' which used to hang in the Sacristy of the Tempio, and is now in the Pinacoteca Comunale, Rimini. 'La Calunnia' by Sandro Botticelli (1444/5–1510) is a late work (*c.*1494) based on Lucian's description of a painting by Apelles. Fra Angelico (*c.*1400–50) painted a number of works in Cortona which Pound recommends in the *Guide to Kulchur*.[92] Ambrogio Praedis (*c.*1455–1517) was a follower of Leonardo da Vinci, but also produced profile portraits which may have been to Pound's taste. So in these lines from Canto XLV the signed column in San Zeno appears at the end of a list of named individuals, Quattrocento painters and sculptors who are thus associated with a medieval craftsman. The link is emphasised by the following lines which instance two French Romanesque churches: 'Not by usura St Trophime / Not by usura Saint Hilaire'.[93] The Quattrocento was a transitional period in which both Ruskin and Pound see the close of one era and the beginning of another. Yet within this phase of decline and fall, there is a marked rise in the social status and aesthetic freedom of the artist. It was a rise which depended upon a clear distinction between the craftsman and the practitioner of an art.

Leon Battista Alberti, the architect of the Tempio, was himself involved in the affirmation of the artist's changing status. Anthony Blunt observed that 'the principal aim of the artists in their claim to be regarded as liberal was to dissociate themselves from the craftsmen';[94] he cites Alberti's *Della Pittura*:

> Before I go any further I think it will be convenient to say whom exactly I mean to call an architect; for I will not set up before you a carpenter and ask you to regard him as the equal of men deeply versed in the other sciences, though it is true that the man who works with his hands serves as an instrument for the architect.[95]

Ezra Pound's sense that there is no significant conflict between the values of San Zeno's Adamo and Leon Battista Alberti may be drawn from that same 'Paris Letter' of 1922; he alludes to the latter as another instance of the healthy past when there was a place for painting and sculpture in the architectural environment:

> Alberti, a very great architect and not particularly well-known painter, says in his praise of painting in the *Trattato della Pittura* that the architect gets his *idea* from the painter, that the painter stirs the desire for beautiful building.[96]

Pound italicises the word 'idea' with good reason; yet it indicates a discrepancy between Alberti's view of architecture and that embodied in the stone-carving of San Zeno. Intimately connected with the elevation of the artist above the craftsman is a distinction drawn between the conception and the execution of building work. It is evident in Alberti's letter of 18 November 1454 to Matteo de' Pasti (*c.*1420–90), who oversaw the Tempio's construction, when the architect writes of his design: 'You can see where the sizes and proportions of the pilasters come from: if you alter something, all that harmony is destroyed.'[97]

Painters who executed decorations for Quattrocento buildings also insisted on their status as practitioners of an art. In his letter of complaint to Borso d'Este of 25 March 1470, Francesco del Cossa 'asserts his superiority over merely artisan painters':[98]

> Let me humbly remind you that I am Francesco del Cossa, who on my own did the three panels on the wall next the anteroom . . . I should be contented and well provided if I were only a manual worker, but the circumstances are very different, and it pains and saddens me. This is especially so because, having now begun to get something of a name, I am treated and judged and compared with the poorest apprentice in Ferrara . . .[99]

What, as well as making a name, allowed an artist to assert his superiority over a manual worker? Canto CXIV contains an answer: 'And the literature of his time (Sandro's, Firenze) was / in painting.'[100] Sandro Botticelli painted works which were derived from literary sources and, for Pound, seem to have constituted the contemporary poetry and prose. The painter is thus the practitioner of a liberal art, rather than an artisan painter, because he realises pleasing and instructing conceptions. He might or might not execute all of his design, depending upon the price paid for his skill or that of his assistants – a practice Michael Baxandall notes 'already gaining ground in the middle of the [fifteenth] century'.[101] The presence of subservient assistants would imply that distinction between conceiving and producing, with the master's status deriving both from his superior skills and his powers of conception.

Sandro Botticelli, 'The Calumny of Apelles', c.1494
photograph: *Mansell Collection*

Leon Battista Alberti's treatise on painting had encouraged artists to attempt a version of Apelles's picture 'aimed at the correction of vice',[102] which is known only from a description of it in Lucian. A comparison of Alberti's account of the picture with Botticelli's painting suggests that Sandro may have followed it closely. D. G. Bridson answers the question why Pound cites this particular late Botticelli in Canto XLV by referring us to Alberti's treatise and then: 'there was much in the concept of *La Calunnia* which must have started thoughts. A righteous man (Innocence) being calumniated and denounced to ass-eared Authority . . . What could better stand for his own dramatisation at Rapallo during the thirties?'[103] I do not think Pound could possibly have associated himself with the naked boy being dragged along by the hair. The 'man with very large ears',[104] though, is identified as Midas by Alberti. The king who could make whatever he touched turn to gold appearing in Botticelli's painting which represents an allegory of misinformation may have suggested to Pound that he mention it in his denunciation of usury's effects. The connection, to Pound's way of thinking, between gold and mendacity is reiterated in Canto LXXVIII: 'and Churchill's return to Midas broadcast by his liary'.[105] A further attraction in the painting is

[145]

suggested by Walter Pater's idea that the same woman may be seen in both 'La Calunnia' and 'La Nascita di Venere':

> The same figure – tradition connects it with Simonetta, the mistress of Giuliano de' Medici – appears . . . again as *Veritas*, in the allegorical picture of *Calumnia*, where one may note in passing the suggestiveness of an accident which identifies the image of Truth with the person of Venus.[106]

True love resists usurious obfuscation: this is one aspect of Pound's theme.

When Vasari writes of 'La Calunnia' that 'Sandro divinely imitated the caprice of that ancient painter',[107] he affirms the Quattrocento artist's liberal status. The stature and fame which made it possible for the artists to negotiate terms with, or complain of ill-treatment by patrons, was encouraged by the association of the painter's role with that of the poet; while the popularity of neo-pagan subjects increased the range of exemplary images a painter or sculptor could undertake. When Pound wrote in Canto XLV that 'with usura / hath no man a painted paradise on his church wall'[108] he seems attracted to the early Catholic Church because of its denunciation of usury; but, in the wider context of the Usura Canto, he prefers the vision of love and man's elevated nature in early Renaissance paganism. The Tempio Malatestiano was so important for him because it eclectically combined aspects of both these values, though, as we shall see, it tended rather towards the heroically pagan.

Leon Battista Alberti, Tempio Malatestiano, 1447–58

The conflicting significance of pagan and Christian images in the art Pound loved is nowhere more crucial than in Sigismondo's Temple. Canto IX concludes:

> 'and built a temple so full of pagan works'
>   i.e. Sigismund
> and in the style 'Past ruin'd Latium'
> The filigree hiding the gothic,
>   with a touch of rhetoric in the whole
> And the old sarcophagi,
>   such as lie, smothered in grass, by San Vitale.[109]

These lines give a succinct view of the Tempio's history and its eclecticism. The first adopts a criticism of the building's interior decoration from the *Commentaries* of Pius II. The Pope excommunicated Sigismondo in December 1460 and had him vilified by declamation on 16 January 1461. Though the Pope was motivated by political rivalry, his objections to the Tempio's paganism are supported by the building itself, which Franco Borsi has described as 'the expression of a cultural world in which religious and pagan values "merge in the fog of a single primordial Christian-philosophical revelation" (Cassirer).'[110] Pound rudely denounces Pius's rude denunciations in Canto X; he does so on cultural and political grounds, for the Pope's opposition to Sigismondo contributed much to his defeat and the stifling of artistic life in Rimini. He does not, however, denounce the Pope's excommunication of Sigismondo on religious grounds, for Pound cannot deny the paganism in the Tempio. Rather, he considers it healthy.

The 'style "Past ruin'd Latium"', Carroll Terrell suggests, echoes a line of Walter Savage Landor's from 'To Ianthe': 'Past ruined Ilion Helen lives' – 'which Pound quotes to align Isotta with the archetypal Helen';[111] it does, however, more directly describe Alberti's classical design for the Tempio. About 1450, when work began on the building, Alberti 'seems to have written the *Descriptio Urbis Romae*, in which he deals with the city's ancient monuments.'[112] Ezra Pound's words 'filigree' and 'a touch of rhetoric' seem to imply a criticism of Alberti's work. The Tempio facade is, strictly, an ornamental agrandissement of the original building – and the distinction between integral and ornamental detail is found central to Pound's distinction between Cavalcanti and Petrarch:

> In Guido the 'figure', the strong metamorphic or 'picturesque' expression is there with purpose to convey or to interpret a definite meaning. In Petrarch it is ornament, the prettiest ornament he could find . . .[113]

As early as *The Spirit of Romance*, Pound had stated a preference for the Romanesque which, with a few specific exceptions, I do not think he subsequently much qualified or renounced: 'the Romanesque architecture, being the natural evolution from the classic, seems more admirable than the artificially classic modes of the Renaissance'.[114] Yet he does not think so badly of the Tempio's exterior because he detects traces of earlier styles in Alberti's building. He accepts the discrepancies of style in the Tempio as necessary when reviewing Adrian Stokes (1902–72), whom he first met in Rapallo in 1926: 'What a medley! The "Tempio" in Rimini would have been a far less daring synthesis had all its details been fully digested and reduced to a unity of style, à la Palladio.'[115] Pound's ability to consider a 'medley' the same as a 'synthesis' indicates much about the kind of unity *The Cantos*, which are often critically defended with the analogy of the Tempio, might display.

Carroll Terrell is not quite accurate, I think, when he notes of the final two lines that 'Pound compares the quiet dignity of the old sarcophagi outside San Vitale to the conglomeration of styles in the Tempio.'[116] First, 'the old sarcophagi' are not the ones actually at San Vitale, but like them: 'such as lie'; these are the ones in the sides of the Tempio. Pound is suggesting that Alberti's design for the side elevation with niched sarcophagi derives from the experience of Byzantine churches in Ravenna. Adrian Stokes, in his early essay 'The Sculptor Agostino di Duccio' (1929), supports Pound's hint of the Byzantine in Alberti:

> As for the influence of Ravenna, although decagonal in shape, the tomb of Theodoric with niches formed by heavy arches rising over a stylobate, may well have suggested the structure of the flanks of the Tempio, especially since it appears that during the Middle Ages those niches were filled by tombs of illustrious persons.[117]

Sigismondo had the remains of Gemisthus Plethon, which he brought back from the Morea after the failure of his campaign there in 1466, buried in one of the Tempio's flanking sarcophagi. Pound encouraged Stokes's interest in Sigismondo's Tempio, and assisted in having his early essays published in *The Criterion*. Donald Davie[118] has examined the influence of Stokes's pre-war volumes

Matteo de' Pasti, reverse of
'Portrait of Sigismondo Malatesta', c.1450
Private Collection

on Pound: especially the affinity of stone and water; the opposition of carving and modelling in sculpture; and the emblematic in Quattro Cento art.

The connection between the Byzantine in Ravenna and the Tempio is further emphasised by Pound's account of how 'Sigismundo got up a few arches, / And stole that marble in Classe, "stole" that is . . .'.[119] The traditional tale of how Malatesta thieved marble from S. Apollinare in Classe, Ravenna, to build his Temple is contradicted by Pound in Canto IX where evidence is offered of a financial transaction. Terrell notes that Pound's insinuation 'is not borne out by the records' and goes on to remark that

> the Tempio incorporates cultural layers from various periods (the Gothic church, the Renaissance shell, the Byzantine marbles), as Pound does in *The Cantos*. Pound's defence of Sigismundo from the charge of stealing is therefore not devoid of a self-serving element.[120]

The separation between 'idea' and 'execution' already mentioned with regard to Alberti's design for the Tempio raises a further matter; Pound notes in his review of Stokes's *Stones of Rimini*:

> Another principle of unity seems to me to exist, and to be given not by the building, but by Pasti's medal of intention.
> I believe the construction to have a spherical basis – fortunately foiled in the effect, but there always as principle and as cause of a solidity, a satisfaction which no other base-form could have attained.[121]

Here Pound happily views Malatesta's failure to complete Alberti's design – which was to include a dome – as giving aesthetic qualities to the building which are instilled from the design, but achieve another effect in its partial execution. This failure then stands as 'a record of courage'. Donald Davie, discussing Venetian builders in Canto XVII, suggests that 'the idea crystallizes only in the process of building, and the achieved building is the only crystallization possible.'[122] This Stokesian interrelation of artist and material fits the achievement of Adamo in San Zeno, or of the Rimini bas-reliefs, but the 'solidity' of the Tempio derives from a discrepancy between preconceived idea and unfinished work. Terrell's association of the eclecticism of the Tempio with that of *The Cantos* implies a view of the long poem as 'a record of courage' rather than 'the only crystallization possible'.

When Pound writes in 'Art and Luxury' that the poet's 'product is immaterial', he means that the work is not a single object:

> In the case of poetry it is the thing itself, not an oleograph or a photo-reproduction which goes to the man on the veldt, to the Ceylon planter, to the errand boy in a Manchester slum.[123]

Yet, the 'thing itself' is 'immaterial'. This should be borne in mind when reading Pound's advice to Mary Barnard on 23 February 1934:

> Thing is to cut a shape in time. Sounds that stop the flow, and durations either of syllables, or implied between them, 'forced onto the voice' of the reader by nature of the 'verse.' (E.g. my *Mauberley*.)[124]

Ezra Pound's sculpting analogy denatures the medium of poetry as much as Pater's '*All art constantly aspires towards the condition of music*'.[125] Pound's aspiring to the condition of sculpture suggests that, while he considers it 'the dignity of the poet'[126] that his work is immaterial, he also sees it as a limitation in the medium, which his desire to conceive of the poem as a thing carved from the language strives to overcome.

Adrian Stokes observes that 'Characteristic of modelling is an effect of the preconceived' and exemplifies the remark by citing the 'all-absorbing rhythm' of 'Bernini, Manet and Rembrandt'. Carving does not display 'so prominent a masterliness, so "wilful" a preconception' and:

> carving entails a dependence, imaginative as well as actual, upon the material that is worked. The stone block attains vivid life under the hand that polishes. Similarly, the shape of the material on which Piero della Francesca and even Giorgione painted, was of the deepest significance to them, far more so than in the case of Rubens, for instance, or of Vermeer.[127]

Gaudier-Brzeska's drawings for the 'Hieratic Head of Ezra Pound', and the photographs of him at work on it, indicate that the final form developed in the process of working the stone; there seems, for example, to have been the idea of diamond eyes at one stage. Thus Gaudier appears to have combined in his work aspects of a powerful preconception with a dependence on working the stone. Emphasis on the substance to be worked in Ruskin, Pound and Stokes aligns the modern sculptor with a craftsmanly aesthetic; but the modern artist's isolation, his independence and obligation to project a personal imaginative conception, place him with the inheritors of an elevation in the artist's status and role which began in the Quattrocento. Similarly, because their subjects are predominantly pagan and astrological, the Tempio's bas-reliefs combine an exultation of the power of human passion in concord with elemental forces – symbolic representations of Sigismondo's love for Isotta – with a Ruskinian, and thus Christian, craftsmanly virtue implied in the subjugation of the artist's will to his material. Pound's poems, and especially *The Cantos*, are records of a struggle between his often wilful preconceptions and an acute sensitivity to the material upon which, at his best, he imaginatively depends.

III Tastes and Judgement

Pier Paolo Pasolini asked in 1968, 'By the way, Pound, which painters have you loved most?' to which he replied, 'I'd say those of the Quattrocento.'[128] Ezra Pound's views on the visual arts are significant both for what they were, and for how he held them. The habits of mind he brought to describing and defending his views represent specific values as much as do the opinions themselves. He made comparisons which see art as representative of political and economic conditions; but he also made others which regarded the political leader as a type of the artist.[129] This is achieved by an impassioned combination of sharp discriminations and broad analogies not only between the different arts, but also diverse cultures and epochs. What Pound attributed to Italian Quattrocento painting and how he advanced his preferences at the expense of other styles will be looked at now, but first I must summarise some of the characteristics of the art he loved.

Pre-eminent among the qualities Pound admired was 'clearly defined outlines' rather than 'muzzy edges'.[130] We can see this in Piero della Francesca's fresco at Rimini (colour plate, p. 30) where the kneeling Sigismondo and his dogs in profile are sharply differentiated from the surrounding space, and from St Sigismund. The combination of clear bounding-lines and delimited areas of colour in paintings such as Botticelli's 'The Birth of Venus' emphasises the separate existences of figures, animals and objects in a world given order by the linear, rhythmic and chromatic coherence of the static design, rather than by the atmosphere's tonally unifying effects – grading also the clarity of objects according to their distance from the viewer's implied position. The relative absence in Quattrocento painting of brushstrokes or signs of working in the paint also attributes independent life to the objects depicted, whereas bravura brushwork such as that of late Titian draws our attention directly to the artist's presence as manipulator of both paint and representation.

In his *Stones of Rimini* review, Pound observes that 'the Rimini bas relief is conceived in three dimensions and then squashed'. Such flattening of the image is a preferred characteristic, which links Quattrocento work with the emphasised picture plane of Vorticist abstraction. The representation of the sea in 'The Birth of Venus' is again illustrative: while the shoreline effectively curves and recedes, the water's surface is not made to seem at right angles to the picture plane, but, especially to the left, appears almost vertical – like a backdrop. Piero della Francesca, with a mathematical linear perspective and central vanishing point, and Giovanni Bellini in his backgrounds and landscape details, could both represent spatial depth: but it is noticeable that the works by them in Rimini lack those characteristics. The similarity of Mantegna's frescoes in Mantua to classical friezes would be another indicative instance, or Pound's preference for Pisanello's

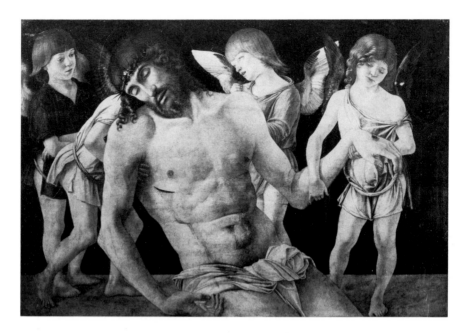

Giovanni Bellini, 'Dead Christ supported by four angels',
before 1468. *Pinacoteca Communale, Rimini*

profile portraiture in medals. This flatness may also be felt in the relative absence of
musculature modelled on limbs, or of deep shadow on the faces portrayed.

Such characteristics contribute to a sense of stillness in these images, distinctly
more marked than in later painting where freer brushwork, deeper modelling of
figures neither profile nor frontal, and dynamic rhythm suggest movement or
action. Leonardo criticised the design of Botticelli's 'Annunciation' for expressing
unsuitable movement: 'Mary, as if desperate, seemed to be trying to throw herself
out of the window.'[131] This may be true of the figure's position, but not of the
manner in which she is painted. Indeed, the shell which carries Venus ashore does
not appear to be moving; the figure to the right representing one of the 'Hours'
about to clothe her in a flowery wrap seems particularly stilled. This motionless-
ness in the way the images are painted suggests attention to a timeless, exemplary
moment: Ludovico Gonzaga meeting Cardinal Francesco Gonzaga; Borso d'Este
administering justice; Sigismondo Malatesta kneeling before his patron saint; or
the crucified Christ supported by four angels. Though Pound calls this last '"the
best Bellini in Italy"'[132] in the *Guide to Kulchur*, he never draws attention to the
religious meaning of the image whose exemplary timelessness affirms Christ's
suffering and his triumph over death. Pater's remarks on Botticelli similarly
under-emphasise Christian content: 'if he painted religious incidents, [he] painted

them with an under-current of original sentiment, which touches you as the real matter of the picture through the veil of its ostensible subject'.[133]

Ezra Pound tends to prefer hieratic and emblematic secular works. Of Piero della Francesca's fresco in the Tempio, Kenneth Clark observes that St Sigismund 'whose plastic, three-quarter pose situates him in a different world . . . is an echo of medieval painting, where the sacred personages were on a higher plane of reality than the detached donors in profile.'[134] This is true, but Sigismondo is firmly in the centre of the painting, and not on a smaller scale. We are to concentrate on the fact that it is *his* piety.

The absence of atmosphere, of aerial perspective, increases both the clarity and timelessness of these works. Yet such eternal stillness is not an image of Christian transcendence for Pound. In 'Painting, Giorgione and Barbaro', another early essay sharing Pound's concerns, Adrian Stokes contrasts an 'out-of-time immediacy' with the 'Dutch and English and Oriental art which troubles the time-sense with hapless distance and homely continuations'. The sunsets of Rubens's late landscapes beautifully combine these two qualities singled out by Stokes for contrastive censure. Stokes also remarks that 'vagueness ever has musical corollaries: thus the silence of a Dutch sunset' and relates the stilled art he loves to 'one of the non-visual arts . . . not to music, but to the immediacy of the poet's image'.[135] We may justly sense Pound's Imagist Manifesto behind this: 'An "Image" is that which presents an intellectual and emotional complex in an instant of time.'[136] Neither feelings of longing nor loss insinuate themselves from the Italian art Pound loved; rather we are confronted with representations of a full presence, which is not thus an image of the Christian creation, but rather of a human sufficiency, a *paradiso terrestre*.

Reviewing Adrian Stokes's *The Quattro Cento* in *The Criterion*, Kenneth Clark notes a danger in passionate art criticism: 'But how hard it is to discriminate without seeming to condemn – no doubt because love is blind.'[137] Ezra Pound, though, did not believe that 'love is blind'; rather that the *Amor* he tries to define in his 'Cavalcanti' stimulates enhanced sight. This capacity to see in an intense, visionary way derives, he claims, from a Mediterranean and non-Christian view of the body: 'The senses at first seem to project for a few yards beyond the body. Effect of a decent climate where a man leaves his nerve-set open . . .'[138] To see the vision of the body that Pound believes to have been extant in Southern Europe, he suggests going to Florence:

Nobody can absorb the *poeti dei primi secoli* and then the paintings of the Uffizi without seeing the relation between them, Daniel, Ventadour, Guido, Sellaio, Botticelli, Ambrogio Praedis, Nic. del Cossa.

All these are clean, all without hell-obsession.[139]

[153]

Pound then makes a number of contrastive observations to explain what he believes happened to this view of the body in painting 'about 1527':

> The people are corpus, corpuscular, but not in the strict sense 'animate', it is no longer the body of air clothed in the body of fire; it no longer radiates, light no longer moves from the eye, there is a great deal of meat, shock absorbing, perhaps – at any rate absorbent.[140]

Here is another effect of usury on art and perception; the 'animate' body would be one in which the physical and the spiritual are indissociable. Kenneth Clark has noticed in nudes by Rubens (1577–1640) and Rembrandt (1606–69) that 'Christian acceptance of the unfortunate body has permitted the Christian privilege of a soul'.[141] If, like Pound, you do not believe in the Christian soul, the material body becomes merely 'corpus' when his version of the 'dissociation of sensibility' occurs.

Why then was this animate vision of the body lost? Pound remarks that 'Loss of values is due usually to lumping and to lack of dissociation. The disproved is thrown out, and the associated, or contemporarily established, goes temporarily with it.'[142] When the theory that light came from the eye was disproved the values that had been associated with it were lost as a lump, he thinks, and he wants to dissociate those values from their basis in primitive physics to preserve them for the present day. His word 'temporarily' is there to tell us that when 'Certain virtues are established'[143] they are never utterly lost, but may be reborn in later centuries.

Pound is at times contemptuous of those artists whose innovations neglected the qualities he valued. When he writes of 'The stupidity of Rubens',[144] for instance, there is in Pound too a 'Loss of values . . . due . . . to lumping and to lack of dissociation', for his injudicious *ad hominem* does not enact the distinction between making a discrimination and the condemnation of something which contrasts with one's own view:

> all that Sandro knew, and Jacopo
> and that Velásquez never suspected
> lost in the brown meat of Rembrandt
> and the raw meat of Rubens and Jordaens
> (Canto LXXX)[145]

The word 'meat' has ambiguities which are being exploited. It appears in the 'Cavalcanti' essay too: 'there is a great deal of meat', and then, 'The dinner scene is more frequently introduced . . .' In the lines from Canto LXXX as well, there is a sardonic analogy implicit between bad oil painting and cookery – the 'raw' and the 'brown'. A possible allusion to Rembrandt's 'The Slaughter Ox' in the Louvre lets us take the word 'meat' literally for a moment; but the comparison

Follower of Botticelli, An Allegory (until 1929 attributed to Jacopo
del Sellaio) called 'Venus reclining with Cupids', after *c.*1485. *Reproduced by
courtesy of The Trustees, The National Gallery, London*

with Botticelli and Jacopo del Sellaio (1442–93) hardens the word's figurative
use. Pound's *Ripostes* (1912) contains 'The Picture' and 'Of Jacopo del Sellaio',
both written about a 'Venus reclining with Cupids' then thought to be by Jacopo. It
is now called 'An Allegory'. D. G. Bridson helpfully points out that 'the picture had
often been regarded as anterior to Botticelli's vastly better *Venus and Mars . . .* and
accordingly much overestimated'.[146] It goes some way to explaining the stark
contrast between the view in Pound's poems –

> The eyes of this dead lady speak to me,
> For here was love, was not to be drowned out

or –

> This man knew out the secret ways of love,
> No man could paint such things who did not know[147]

and that of the National Catalogue: 'It is by some feeble imitator of Botticelli, and
seems to be partly derived from his *Venus and Mars . . .*' which also suggests that
'some allegory of Fertility is intended'.[148] From both these sources, however, we
are encouraged to think that the lines from Canto LXXX, as well as distinguishing
between paintings with 'clean' and those with 'muzzy edges', also discriminate
between attitudes to love and the female body.

We might contrast Botticelli's 'The Birth of Venus', or the anonymous 'An

[155]

Allegory', with nudes such as Rembrandt's 'Bathsheba' in the Louvre, or 'La Pelisse', Rubens's portrait of Hélène Fourment wearing a fur wrap, in Vienna. When 'meat' is read in this context, Pound's Botticellian taste suggests a curiously fastidious attitude to actual bodies. If 'meat' is of a piece with 'The stupidity of Rubens', then the element of recoil, of revulsion in Pound's lines indicates that the word, reacting to these representations, performs the loss of value which it seeks to characterise. It is the word 'meat' which devalues the flesh, not necessarily the painters themselves, or, affecting them, the Reformation or the climate in Belgium and Holland or the tolerance of usury.[149] Moreover, the poet devalues the body by lowering himself to an abusive term. He is himself devalued. Such is the fate of condemnatory language which seeks, by negative definitions, to promote or maintain an embattled value.

Early in his career, Pound had responded to the presence of sentient, reflective, individual people in Rembrandt's work. In 'The Wisdom of Poetry' (1912), he wrote:

> With Rembrandt we are brought to consider the exact nature of things seen, to consider the individual face, not the conventional or type face which we may have learned to expect on canvas.[150]

Comparing this remark with the 'brown meat' line above, I sense in Pound's writings on art two conflicting tendencies: the inclusive and the excluding. In the former, he views the art as a whole and seeks to relate different styles within it by mutually instructive contrasts; in the latter, he applies a prescriptive principle to the various exhibits and divides the 'clean' from the 'muzzy'. In January 1939 he concluded an article on 'René Crevel' with: 'By rough analogy Ribera and the Seicento looked at dresses and draperies; Simone Memmi at his whole subject.'[151] Or, in 'A Visiting Card' (1942), he wrote, 'an expert, looking at a painting (by Memmi, Goya, or any other), should be able to determine the degree of tolerance of usury in the society in which it was painted'.[152] In both these instances qualities are being used primarily and narrowly as symptoms. Further, 'By rough analogy' suggests that the two tendencies (the inclusive, and the excluding) are each supported by habits of mind that derive from the other. Broad association of figures and styles helps to align qualities when Pound wants to separate off other works, while a tempered separation of qualities is required to prevent the inclusive from being a mere lumping together.

In 'I Gather the Limbs of Osiris' (1911–12), Pound distinguishes between the 'man, ignorant of painting, taken into a room containing a picture by Fra Angelico, a picture by Rembrandt, one by Velasquez, Memling, Rafael, Monet, Beardsley, Hokusai, Whistler' who is filled with confusion, attracted by some, repelled by others, and the 'specialist, a man thoroughly trained in some other branch of knowledge' who will

> realise that there are a number of devices, all designed for more or less the same end, none 'better', none 'worse', all different. Each, perhaps, slightly more fit for use under certain conditions for certain objects minutely differentiated.[153]

There are a number of implicit problems in this observation, though it represents a fine open-mindedness in contrast to some of Pound's other utterances on the subject. First, though the implications of the passage are that Pound is an instance of the 'specialist', we have already found him writing as one 'attracted by some, repelled by others'; then the specialist's unconcern for what is better or worse seems not only disingenuous but also practically impossible, a pointless exercise. Pound was always, in his terms, both a 'man, ignorant of painting' but with strong responses or reactions, and a 'specialist . . . in some other branch of knowledge' seeking to identify the differences between styles. If the second of these was tempering the former, he could write inclusive and evaluative criticism; if the former was dominant it would be polemic which seemed to exclude styles or artists upon a prescriptive principle. Further, by imagining that they were two separate categories, he risked mistaking the one for the other: imagining that a sharp attitude was an objective discrimination.

Pound's recollections of the paintings by Diego Velasquez (1599–1660) in the Prado, which he saw in 1906, show these conflicting tendencies at work. In the line from Canto LXXX, 'and that Velásquez never suspected', Pound evidently considers the Spanish painter a cut above his near contemporaries from the Low Countries. In 1917, perhaps reminded of them by the visit to London of Father José Maria de Elizondo whom he had met in Madrid, Ezra Pound praised T. S. Eliot's *Prufrock and other Observations* by noting:

> If it is permitted to make comparison with a different art, let me say that he has used contemporary detail very much as Velasquez used contemporary detail in *Las Meninas*; the cold gray-green tones of the Spanish painter have, it seems to me, an emotional value not unlike the emotional value of Mr Eliot's rhythms, and of his vocabulary.[154]

Pound's 'If it is permitted', 'let me say', and 'it seems to me' all bespeak a man that moves with care and proportion as regards both his readers and the suggestive but entirely illustrative comparison he is advancing.

A manuscript from 1929, now published in *Ezra Pound and the Visual Arts*, finds him recalling the 1906 visits – 'if not daily at least with great frequency . . . finding each day something worth thinking about' – but after which he notes:

At the same time I still really prefer Carpaccio, and the Bellini in Rimini, and Piero Francesca and in general paintings with clearly defined outlines to any with muzzy edges. I know why these clean edges will not serve for all painting. This however is my personal angle.[155]

Emphasis here is firmly on the artist's technique rather than an economic or political principle, and it is upon Pound's taste rather than any 'objective' discrimination. We can hear him being both a man with preferences, and a specialist who appreciates that the artists developed their techniques to achieve different ends.

Again, in 1937, Pound devoted a page to the Prado paintings (they are recalled once more in the opening movements of Cantos LXXX and LXXXI) and added:

A dozen returns and each time a new permanent acquisition, light, green shadows instead of the brown as in Rembrandt, who has steadily declined through 30 years in his power to rouse enthusiasm. I don't mean ceased, I mean that the current in our past three decades has been toward the primitives, WITH a forward current, via Velasquez . . .[156]

Here, in the *Guide to Kulchur*'s improvised prose, the tendencies to inclusive comparison and excluding judgement are vying for supremacy, and Pound's style shows signs of being unequal to the tussle. The preference for green to brown shadow seems impelled by more than colouristic considerations which remain unexpressed, and it has some of the pejorative force of 'brown meat'. Declining powers are attributed to the art work, while the viewer's openness to being roused is never in question. Yet Pound's 'I don't mean ceased' attempts a degree of inclusive balance, but does sound like a compensatory second thought; his 'the current in our past three decades' is a preference in the guise of a general trend; and his 'WITH a forward current' seems a further example of over-emphatic short-hand calling out for more complex analysis and articulation than there is any time for. Here, with currents flowing in both directions, Pound seems caught between two aesthetic loyalties that he has come to feel represent conflicting values in a struggle against usury where he must take sides; but still he would prefer not to give up his memories of Velasquez, for to do that would be to renounce the experience of art for an attitude about it.

D. G. Bridson's remark that the discriminations made in 'all that Sandro knew . . .' are 'no more than Pound's preference . . .'[157] seems least satisfactory if applied to Canto XLV, which Bridson knows to be 'attacking the stultifying effects of usury' where we may suppose that he 'instances the most outstanding art which could be stultified.'[158] Canto XLV lists works whose 'cleanly defined outlines' exemplify a mode of vision that 'came not by usura', but Pound does not say there whether the art of an epoch, by showing certain aesthetic properties, can resist the tolerance of usury that is said to corrupt draftsmanship: 'with usura the line grows thick / with usura is no clear demarcation'.[159] Is art the passive receiver of cultural conditions, registering them so that 'an expert' can 'determine the degree of tolerance of usury in the society in which it was painted'? Or may the artist draw a line somewhere? If the latter is true, the former cannot be, because individual pieces would show varying degrees of tolerance depending on how actively resistant the particular artist's work were. Yet if the former is true, artists are powerless to do more than reflect the degree of tolerance in the society. When Pound is diagnosing cultural decay, he seems to believe that artists are powerless to resist; but, when thinking of his insights and his poetic technique, they appear able actively to oppose debilitating cultural conditions.

In the *Guide to Kulchur* he states: 'A tolerance of gombeen men and stealers of harvest by money, by distortion and dirtiness, runs concurrent with a fattening in all art forms' and asserts: 'I have not deflected a hair's breadth from my lists of beautiful objects, made in my own head and held before I ever thought of usura as a murrain and a marasmus.'[160] Saying this implies that his instincts are healthy, uninfected by the centuries of usurious lending; you could not 'determine the degree of tolerance of usury' in Canto XLV: 'Duccio came not by usura / nor Pier della Francesca; Zuan Bellin' not by usura . . .'[161] That 'current in our past three decades', which shows in a preference for the primitives listed above, is a counter-current working against the concurrence of usury and 'fattening in all art-forms'. Sigismondo Malatesta

> had a little of the best there in Rimini. He had perhaps Zuan Bellin's best bit of painting. He had all he cd. get of Pier della Francesca. Federigo Urbino was his Amy Lowell . . . Malatesta managed *against* the current of power.[162]

Pound italicises the word to let us know that the cultural trend of which he is a part in this century is allied with Sigismondo Malatesta's role as an art patron. The association of Amy Lowell with Federigo Urbino is a 'rough analogy' indeed, and, since the American poetess had usurped Pound's role as leader of the Imagist movement and 'with more wealth got the seconds', an equally rough analogy would seem to imply that Pound is identifying himself with his hero Sigismondo Malatesta. Pound's weakness for seeing the present in terms of the past can be felt as benign in his recollection of Gaudier-Brzeska at work, 'this head "out of the renaissance."' Yet his tendency to understand the present by analogies drawn from history, and vice-versa, also fostered this, to me, more pernicious association in a letter of 18 February 1932 to John Drummond:

> Don't knock Mussolini, at least not until you have weighed up the obstacles

and necessities of the time. He will end with Sigismundo and the men of order, not with the pus-sacks and destroyers.[163]

This analogy recurs a number of times in *The Pisan Cantos*, written after Mussolini's defeat and death; his reiteration of the 'fanciful kinship' asks us to consider the furthest ends to which Ezra Pound could put the works of Italian art he loved.

IV Reiteration and Resurgence in The Pisan Cantos

In 'Fragments of an Atmosphere', Mary de Rachewiltz, Pound's daughter by Olga Rudge, the American violinist, cites her father's radio broadcast 'James Joyce: to his Memory' – 'Now I have no more GIVEN myself to fascism . . . than I have given myself to Mr Joyce'. And he defends his political involvement by referring critics to 'a line from the Malatesta Cantos'[164] which actually reads:

> books, arms,
> And men of unusual genius,
> Both of ancient times and our own . . .[165]

The lines describe the topics of Sigismondo Malatesta's conversation, and Pound is comparing his own involvement in politics and culture with such exalted talk. It is an unconvincing retort to critics because its broad associations create a severe confusion of categories and contexts. Might we not distinguish in kind between literary promotion, such as Pound's for Joyce, in war or peace, and advocacy such as Pound's for Mussolini in war rather than peace? Similarly there may seem a temporal and territorial distinction to be drawn between the discussion of war and culture by a *condottiero* in the fifteenth century, and by an American poet broadcasting from Rome in World War II. After quoting the lines from Canto XI describing '"in short the usual subjects / Of conversation between intelligent men"', Pound remarks that 'As a writer I am given to no one and to all men.' In *The Pisan Cantos*, are Pound's cultural and aesthetic interests, from which he draws analogies including his interpretations of Mussolini, 'above warring factions'?[166] Or do his analogies between the art he loves and his political ideals enlist the cultural objects into an engaged position within the war's factions? When, in *The Pisan Cantos*, Pound lovingly remembers his 'true heritage' in a lifetime of aesthetic allegiances, is his culture part of a resurgent humanism, or are Pound's loves being polemically marshalled against the Allied armies in Italy?

On the first page of Canto LXXIV, the 'clear demarcation' of Canto XLV becomes: 'a precise definition / transmitted thus Sigismundo / thus Duccio, thus Zuan

Bellin . . .' That repeated 'thus', like 'Thus Ben and la Clara *a Milano*',[167] seems the remnant of a condensed proposition expressing an alliance in Pound's mind between aesthetic and political forces which opposed the usurocracy, and which that supposed conspiracy had tried to destroy. The dead bodies of Benito Mussolini and his mistress, Claretta Petacci, were strung up and abused in Piazzale Loreto, Milan. Pound's lines lead into an attack on 'Churchillian' economics and his return to the gold standard in 1925. The 'precise definition' is that clear line in Agostino di Duccio's stone-carving, or Bellini's 'Cristo Morto Sorretto da Quattro Angeli', both, of course, in Rimini. The Tempio Malatestiano had been hit by Allied bombing on 28 December 1943 and 29 January 1944. Pound may have thought it had been totally destroyed, though later he seems to imply that the frontage had been severely damaged:

> and the clouds over the Pisan meadows
> > are indubitably as fine as any to be seen
> from the peninsula
> > ογ βάρβαροι have not destroyed them
> > as they have Sigismundo's Temple[168]

– 'hoi barbaroi', the barbarians (or Allied bombers) could not destroy the clouds. For Ezra Pound in 1945 what had threatened the Italian art he loved was the Allied invasion of Italy. It had also precipitated Mussolini's fall from power in 1943. Within *The Pisan Cantos*, Pound tries to present what he believes to be evidence for a pre-war conspiracy to overthrow the Duce, engineered by British industrial interests. Once again, the analogy with Sigismondo Malatesta is implicit in the juxtaposition:

> and the best de la Robbia busted to flinders
>
> . . .
>
> and the front of the Tempio, Rimini
> It will not take uth twenty yearth
> > to cwuth Mutholini
> and the economic war has begun[169]

The remark Pound cites here in Canto LXXX is reported as being made by the brother of the head of Imperial Chemicals (ICI) at the time of Mussolini's war in Abyssinia, when in October 1935 the League of Nations imposed sanctions on Italy.

The aesthetic ideal of the 'precise definition' associates a Confucian principle of sincerity, clarity in design or stone-carving, and the accurate use of words; it also helped foster political wishful thinking about Mussolini at Salò. The 'Verona Manifesto', Mussolini's policy document for the Fascist Social Republic, published in November 1943, appears in Canto LXXVIII. Pound, recalling his own sojourn by Lake Garda at about that time, believed the discrimination of rights 'to' property from rights 'of' property indicated the survival of his political hero's wisdom and good intentions:

> 'alla' non 'della' in il Programma di Verona
>> the old hand as stylist still holding its cunning
>> and the water flowing away from that side of the lake
>> is silent as never at Sirmio
>>> under the arches
>> Foresteria, Salò, Gardone
>>> to dream the Republic.[170]

Rather it indicates the survival of Pound's will to believe; in 1933 he had written 'Any thorough judgment of MUSSOLINI will be in measure an act of faith . . .'[171] Denis Mack Smith in his *Mussolini* argues that 'the "Verona Manifesto" was mainly window-dressing'.[172] Pound's lines recalling the lake water present another value strictly incompatible with the Duce's 'cunning' old hand – though Pound associates them. Canto LXXIV also has a memory of Salò, where 'the water was still on the west side' and 'in the stillness outlasting all wars/"La Donna" said Nicoletti . . .'[173] Pound links together water, women ('La Donna') and a stillness more permanent than war because they attribute a timelessness to Mussolini's political example – as understood by the poet at this time. Mussolini's love is memorialised in the phrase 'Ben and la Clara', and we may detect in *The Pisan Cantos* analogous loves: Sigismondo's for Isotta, and Pound's for Olga Rudge.[174]

The association of women and water through the influence of the moon is central to Adrian Stokes's interpretation of the Tempio bas-reliefs:

> Agostino's stone forms, luminous and swimming on the stone reduplicate Isotta's magnetism to which Sigismondo was, or wished to think he was, subject. Like the planetary orbits, her powers exercised him. She was the huntress Moon. . .

For Stokes, 'Isotta is Diana, is Mercury, is Venus, one above the other in the Tempio' and he speculates on why Sigismondo needed or wanted such emblems in his church, concluding, 'because he truly loved Isotta and felt the goddess in her'.[175] The passage quoted from above, where Pound records the bombing of Sigismondo's Temple by 'hoi barbaroi', continues by invoking 'Divae Ixottae (and as to her effigy that was in Pisa?)' and ends by beautifully sending word to his own:

> O white-chested martin, God damn it,
>> as no one else will carry a message,
>> say to La Cara: amo.[176]

Recurrently throughout *The Pisan Cantos*, Ezra Pound calls upon memories of Botticelli's 'The Birth of Venus' and Agostino di Duccio's bas-reliefs of Venus and Diana in the Tempio (colour plate, p.31). He wants the vision of a composite female goddess to inspire him and to aid in the transmutation of his constricting environs: these Quattrocento representations of women are to assist him to 'Elysium, though it were in the halls of hell'.[177]

Donald Davie[178] has discussed the analogies between sexual relations and stone-carving which lie behind these lines from Canto LXXIV:

> stone knowing the form which the carver imparts it
> the stone knows the form
> sia Cythera, sia Ixotta, sia in Santa Maria dei Miracoli
>   where Pietro Romano has fashioned the bases . . .[179]

'Cythera' is the goddess Venus, and it is through further reiterations of Pound's habitual analogies that we move via Isotta degli Atti to the carved mermaids – in fact by Pietro Lombardo in the 'jewel box', Santa Maria dei Miracoli, Venice; there the Stokesian associations of stone and water ('mermaids, that carving'[180]) are again implicit. The linking of such images to Botticelli's Venus occurs later in the same canto and in contexts where Olga Rudge is also being remembered. Pound's daughter, Mary de Rachewiltz,[181] sees her mother in the 'rosy-fingered' dawn:

> Beloved the hours βροδοδάκτυλος
>   as against the half-light of the window
>   with the sea beyond making horizon
> le contre-jour the line of the cameo
> profile 'to carve Achaia'
>   a dream passing over the face in the half-light
>   Venere, Cytherea 'aut Rhodon'
>   vento ligure, veni . . .[182]

That phrase '"to carve Achaia"' is an altered allusion to *Hugh Selwyn Mauberley*. Two pages later in Canto LXXIV, there is another passing memory: '. . . cheek bone, by verbal manifestation,/her eyes as in "La Nascita"'.[183] Pound is imagining Botticelli's 'La Nascita di Venere' set in Liguria, where the Ligurian wind brings her ashore. Both these passages, while visualising Olga Rudge as Venus, recall the combination of aesthetic and sexual criticism meted out to Hugh Selwyn Mauberley and his '"fundamental passion"'.[184]

In the second part of *Hugh Selwyn Mauberley* the aesthete dramatised there, though he shares many of Pound's tastes in the arts, fails to achieve any major work because he responds to those artefacts with an asexual delectation. Mauberley is a 'Colourless/Pier Francesca' or a 'Pisanello lacking the skill/To forge Achaia'.[185] Pound uses 'forge' with an intended ambiguity on 'counterfeit'. His poem is an identification and renunciation of qualities in his own art that by 1920 he had come to consider limiting. In *The Pisan Cantos*, however, he returns to the aesthetic ideal expressed in the earlier poem, but emphatically implies his superior passion and love of womankind. In Canto LXXX we re-encounter the Venus of Agostino's bas-relief combined with a memory of his Diana standing upon a scythe-like moon: 'Cythera, in the moon's barge whither? / how hast thou the crescent for car?'[186] A page later, just before the 'all that Sandro knew' lines, the goddess Venus is referred to again and 'as a leaf borne in the current'.[187] This phrase recurs in Canto LXXXI before the 'libretto' section as 'a leaf in the current / at my grates no Althea'.[188] Here, most beautifully, Pound associates himself with the Cavalier poet Richard Lovelace who laments from prison the absence of his love. It is thus crucially important that a real woman is hinted at as the actual instance of pagan divinity for Pound, because it fends off the association with that poor English failure, Hugh Selwyn Mauberley

> – Given that is his 'fundamental passion,'
> This urge to convey the relation
> Of eye-lid and cheek-bone
> By verbal manifestation;
>
> To present the series
> Of curious heads in medallion –
>
> He had passed, inconscient, full gaze,
> The wide-banded irides
> And botticellian sprays implied
> In their diastasis;
>
> Which anaesthesis, noted a year late,
> And weighed, revealed his great affect,
> (Orchid), mandate
> Of Eros, a retrospect.[189]

Pound's reliance on sexual love as the inspiration and light of art, like all positive values, is susceptible to over-emphasis and misapplication. Towards the end of Canto LXXXIV, referring to Alessandro Pavolini, Fernando Mezzasoma and Mussolini, Pound attributes by association 'humanitas (manhood)'[190] to them. The bracketed interpretation makes those three leaders of the Salò Republic into instances of Pound's ideal men, an ideal which derives analogical support, as we have seen, from the unfaltering absence of diffidence in a man's will and his sexuality. To take such men as instances of manhood is fatally to confuse passionate strength with the fear of weakness that can exploit violence as an arm of political policy.[191] Yet Ezra Pound adopts these flawed characters for archetypal figures, as if they were emblems of good government from a Quattrocento fresco-cycle; and, in *The Pisan Cantos*, the poet had such a cycle in mind.

'Yeats and his wife George so liked Rapallo when they went there for Yeats's health that in February 1928 they decided to take a flat there',[192] Noel Stock tells us; one result of this stay was W. B. Yeats's small book 'A Packet for Ezra Pound', later adopted as the opening for *A Vision*. It contains a suggestion about the structure of *The Cantos* that has exercised Pound's critics for some time. In the form of a reported conversation between the two poets, Yeats introduced the idea that the structural principle of his long poem could be understood by analogies from music, the fugue, and painting – by looking at the frescoes in the Palazzo Schifanoia, Ferrara. Pound was projecting a long poem with a tripartite structure, and behind it we must always suppose the ideal of Dante's *Divine Comedy*. Yeats describes the three levels of the frescoes and correlates them with aspects of Pound's poem; these aspects are signified by groups of letters because they are to represent not static subjects but elements that can be interwoven and recur:

> He has shown me upon the wall a photograph of a Cosimo Tura decoration in three compartments, in the upper the Triumph of Love and the Triumph of Chastity, in the middle Zodiacal signs, and in the lower certain events in Cosimo Tura's day. The Descent and Metamorphosis – ABCD and JKLM – his [Pound's] fixed elements, took the place of the Zodiac, the archetypal persons – XYZ – that of the Triumphs, and certain modern events – his letters that do not recur – that of those events in Cosimo Tura's day.[193]

Cosimo Tura (*c.*1430–95) was throughout his career court painter to Borso d'Este and his successor Ercole I. He worked on the Schifanoia frescoes with Ercole de' Roberti and Francesco del Cossa. There has been some scholarly uncertainty about who executed the sections for March and April (colour plate, p.32) which Pound had in reproduction; at various points in *The Cantos* he attributes them to Cosimo Tura and del Cossa. Pound's photograph was of the east wall,[194] which displays decorations for the months of March, April and May. From Yeats's account it appears that Pound had an illustration of March and April; this is confirmed by Pound's recalling them in *The Pisan Cantos*, for the figures 'at Schifanoja under the Ram and Bull'[195] appear in the lowest level of the tripartite designs for those months.

In the highest panel for March is the Triumph of Minerva; on the left of her is a group of writers, magistrates and legal advisers; on the right, women engaged in weaving, embroidering, cutting and sewing. The central section shows the Ram

Francesco del Cossa, 'March', Palazzo Schifanoia, Ferrara, 1470

surmounted by a female figure representing Spring or Wisdom; to the left, a figure depicting Laziness; to the right, another of Activity. In the lowest panel are scenes showing figures tending a trellis, a hunt, and Borso d'Este administering justice. April is represented by, at the top, the Triumph of Venus with pairs of lovers on both sides of her. The Zodiac sign is the Bull surmounted by a man holding the key to Spring in his hand; to the left are figures showing Maternal Felicity; to the right, a representation of Dissoluteness. At the bottom are displayed a *palio* (or horse race), departure for the hunt, and Borso giving money to his clown Scocola. Art historians now seem largely in agreement that these decorations are by Francesco del Cossa; their date is probably approximately 1470.[196]

The first mention of the Schifanoia Frescoes appears in Canto XXIV devoted to incidents in the history of the Este family. The conclusion to Canto III with its allusion to Mantegna's Gonzaga Frescoes is echoed by this canto's indication that neglect and decay were also to be the fate of these works before more recent restorations and scholarly interest:

> "Albert made me, Tura painted my wall,
> And Julia the Countess sold to a tannery . . ."[197]

Borso d'Este is one of *The Cantos'* archetypal figures; Canto XX closes with his father's urging 'Peace! / Borso . . . , Borso!', which is picked up in the next canto's opening: 'Keep the peace, Borso!'[198] He is being urged by Niccolò d'Este to maintain the stability and prosperity of Ferrara through peaceful co-existence with neighbouring states. The Schifanoia Frescoes celebrate him in the lowest panels, though their representation of harmony between human, natural, and astrological order would also implicitly praise his ordering influence. Nevertheless, Pound's substituting the archetypal persons for the Triumphs is – if Yeats is right – a tendentious reinterpretation of the relations between one level of the fresco and another.

In *The Barb of Time* Daniel Pearlman tries with some success to convince his readers that the frescoes' schema corresponds to the vision of Time, as he finds it, in Cantos I–LXXXIV, adding helpfully:

> It is tempting to think that Pound conceived of the design of his poem in direct consequence of his exposure to the frescoes, but 'Pound has explicitly said that he came upon the Tura frescoes after the poem was well under way, and found there not a source but a confirmation of his procedures.'[199]

Pearlman is quoting from an unpublished letter of Hugh Kenner's, whose word 'confirmation' rather begs the question of how an analogy drawn from a fresco can confirm a poetic procedure. More recently critics have warned against assuming a rigid tripartite schema to *The Cantos*, and such scepticism implies doubts about the aptness of the analogy from the Schifanoia Frescoes. Recalling Yeats's explanation, it is true that Canto I is a descent, and Canto II a metamorphosis; the Malatesta Cantos present an archetypal person; and Canto XVI events of Pound's day (World War I and the Russian Revolution). Nevertheless, the organisation of large groups of cantos, or of material within a canto, cannot usefully be related to the frescoes because the static, spatial organisation of a wall decoration presents its order all at once; but a poem such as *The Cantos* has an order which evolved only as it was being written.

In Canto LXXIV, when whatever development Pound had had in mind for his work had been permanently diverted by the war and its aftermath for the poet, a sense of order neither static nor predictable is recognised and reinforced by recalling Botticelli's 'The Birth of Venus', but as if from within the action:

> but this air brought her ashore a la marina
> with the great shell borne on the seawaves
> > nautilis biancastra
> By no means an orderly Dantescan rising
> but as the winds veer . . .[200]

Although *The Pisan Cantos* have a fluctuating and uncertain direction, unlike Dante's *Divine Comedy*, Pound had developed habits of association and analogy with which the reader becomes familiar. When he substitutes the archetypal figures for the Triumphs in Yeats's account of the Schifanoia Frescoes, the implication is that these figures will represent ideals that survive the passage of time, will indeed exemplify timeless values, like Chastity or Love. Yet, in the light of Pound's attachment to Mussolini, we find that unlike Chastity or Love the historical and political interpretation of Pound's archetypal figures remains open, however surely placed they may appear in *The Cantos*. Do the archetypal figures like Mussolini represent qualities that could be said to transcend their time, or should they be with the 'letters that do not recur' in history, or the history of modern times?

The significance of the Schifanoia Frescoes for Pound's poem is complicated in *The Pisan Cantos* where there are five brief allusions to them. The first two, towards the end of Canto LXXVII, compare the negro soldiers in the Detention Training Centre near Pisa, Pound's immediate vicinity, with the figures of country labourers in the fresco's lowest section representing March. They are painted with deeply sun-tanned skins, which, with their labourers' clothes in nondescript colours, may have suggested the affinity to Pound:

> – niggers comin' over the obstacle fence
> as in the insets at the Schifanoja
> (del Cossa) to scale, 10,000 gibbet-iform posts supporting
> barbed wire . . . [201]

The fencing of the Pisa Detention Training Centre resembled, for Pound, a trellis. His invention 'gibbet-iform' and also the 'barbed wire' register a discrepancy between the ordered ideal life of the frescoes and military order of the camp. Yet it is the words 'to scale' that are picked up and emphasised in the next allusion: 'men move to scale   as in Del Cossa's insets / at Schifanoja under the Ram and Bull'.[202] The figures in the frescoes, and by association those in Pound's environs, are 'to scale' because they are under the Zodiac signs, placed in relation to planetary influences, and because they fit their physical environment: they are between the earth and sky. Later references support these implications. Early in Canto LXXVIII Pound sees the soldiers' uniforms as harmonious with the Italian scenery:

> and those negroes by the clothes-line are extraordinarily like the
> figures del Cossa
> Their green does not swear at the landscape . . . [203]

Canto LXXIX opens with a further recollection: 'Moon, cloud, tower, a patch of the battistero all of a whiteness, / dirt pile as per the Del Cossa inset'.[204] Here another effect in recalling the frescoes may be felt, for they help to co-ordinate elements of the poet's surroundings. This co-ordination takes place on two planes, though, and introduces separable issues:

> whereas the sight of a good nigger is cheering
> the bad'uns wont look you straight
> Guard's cap quattrocento passes *a cavallo*
> on horseback through landscape Cosimo Tura
> or, as some think, Del Cossa;[205]

Pound's analogy helps organise the elements of his scenery on a spatial plane, making a putative landscape description of the DTC and its environs, and implicitly locating the poet within his context; it also occasions judgments of quality, value and degree by Pound with regard to his situation – suggested perhaps by the tripartite ordering of the Ferrara frescoes.

The character of Pound's judgments is affected by his being within the situation that he evaluates. He wrote a brief explanation of what his new cantos contained to the DTC censor: 'The form of the poem and main progress is conditioned by its own inner shape, but the life of the DTC passing OUTSIDE the scheme cannot but

[169]

impinge, or break into the main flow'.[206] It would be wrong to take this as a statement which described accurately either Pound's intentions or what he felt he had achieved. The sentence is strikingly equivocal about whether the form of the poem derives from 'inner shape' or from a 'scheme', which must derive from without. Similarly, is the DTC in the poem or not? To say it impinges suggests that it influences the poem without necessarily getting into it, to say 'break into' is unequivocal, but implies violent effort on the part of the external situation, as if the Detention Training Centre were a series of unwanted interruptions. The Schifanoia Frescoes and the negro soldiers are important because they exemplify both the presence of thought about 'scheme' in the poem, and, sponsored by the impinging soldiers, break into the main flow. They instance a scheme that the main flow has been thought to display, and they serve to interrupt it. Yet, more accurately, the negro soldiers are elements in the landscape of the camp which impinge on the flow of the poet's thoughts, and the memory of the Schifanoia Palace then seems to attempt two things: it would compose the impingement of an external world by relating it to the static order of a painting; it would locate that impinging reality within a scale of values governed by the Triumph of Love or Chastity in the frescoes and that of archetypal figures in the poem. The negroes might thus be seen as part of the events of Pound's day that do not recur.

Pietro Lombardo, Mermaids,
detail, Santa Maria dei Miracoli, Venice

Ezra Pound appears personally as well as physically isolated from the negro soldiers, but his poem expresses gratitude to some of them for acts of kindness and implies a degree of fellow-feeling. Their association by Pound with the figures in the Schifanoia Frescoes might appear to be a means of ordering them, at least putatively, into the fluctuations of his poem. There is, however, one more effect of the comparison, for the soldiers of the DTC are given a dignity and significance in Pound's field of vision that they might well not otherwise have had. Their effect is thus itself equivocal. The poet's illusions, his errors of judgment about politics and economics are interrupted by the 'life of the DTC' – and he has the technical flexibility to respond to this life passing outside which 'cannot but impinge'. The Schifanoia Frescoes were an example to Pound of how the world of others' lives could be represented within a large, complex and fluctuating order. There is evidence in *The Pisan Cantos* for supposing that this is what Pound believed or hoped he was achieving. Yet the discontinuous, fragmentary syntax of his poetic method made it very difficult for him to articulate and sustain judgments or embody the values that would have been required for such a perhaps insuperable task. I think it is fortunate that he did not approach that achievement, for, at moments such as the impingement of the black soldiers climbing the barbed wire, Pound's fragmentary technique manages to register something of the irreducible and unforeseen reality of his situation.

As a counter to the confusions of his own mind on those subjects which oppressed him with a sense of the world's injustice, this presentation of his predicament breaking into the main flow exemplifies the resurgence of an instinctual poetic strength more resilient than any that his scheme of opinions and habits of mind might and would try to reiterate within *The Pisan Cantos*. In 'Wyndham Lewis at the Goupil' (1919) Pound's praise for Lewis's war pictures also characterises both the conflicting pressures on war art, and the endurance that art arising out of that conflict would at best exemplify. Lewis's works

> are the best art that has 'come out of the war'; but they have come a good deal more out of art; out of art's resistance to war, than out of war's much-vaunted 'effect upon art.' Indeed, Mr. Lewis would seem to suggest that art is a cut above war; that art might even outlast it.[207]

Pound's involvement with Mussolini does not, however much Pound thought it might, exemplify a resistance to war. Yet *The Pisan Cantos* 'come a good deal more out of art', and to that extent contradict their own reiterated polemical confusions.

Interrogated at Genoa in the spring of 1945, Pound stated: 'I have at all times opposed certain grey zones of the Fascist opportunism by defining fascism in a way to make it fit my own views.'[208] This use of the word 'fascism' does not exemplify 'a precise definition' but rather Adrian Stokes's modelling sculptor who projects a preconception on to his material. Passages in *The Pisan Cantos* instance Pound having his way with words. Yet Donald Davie is right to affirm of these cantos that

> Only when he sees stone in and for itself, the artist's working of it only a drawing out of what was latent in the stone to begin with – only then, as in the sculptures of S. Maria dei Miracoli in Venice, can it save him . . .[209]

What Davie says of stone here is also, at times, true of the poet's medium; and that admirable imaginative dependence on words in Pound's best work is also fostered by his preferences in architecture, painting, and sculpture. Fortunately throughout *The Pisan Cantos* and elsewhere in his long poem Ezra Pound remembered the works of art he loved.

Notes

1 *Gaudier-Brzeska: a Memoir* (New York, 1970), p.48.
2 An instance of Pound's efforts to ameliorate the conditions of artists he admired may be found in the story of his relations with the American art collector John Quinn; see, for a selection of Pound's correspondence with Quinn, *Ezra Pound and the Visual Arts*, ed. Harriet Zinnes (New York, 1980), pp.229–46.
3 Wyndham Lewis, *Time and Western Man* (London, 1927), p.87.
4 Joseph Hone, *W. B. Yeats* (London, 1942), pp.265 and 267.
5 W. B. Yeats, *Collected Poems* (London, 1950), p.120.
6 *Literary Essays of Ezra Pound*, ed. T. S. Eliot (London, 1954), p.379.
7 *Gaudier*, p.45.
8 *Collected Shorter Poems* (London, 1984), p.159; and see Peter Brooker, *A Student's Guide to the Selected Poems of Ezra Pound* (London, 1979), pp.108–9.
9 Yeats, *Collected Poems*, p.169.
10 *Ibid.*
11 *Ibid.*, pp.169–70.
12 *Literary Essays*, p.220.
13 *Ibid.*
14 See Ezra Pound and Dorothy Shakespear, *Their Letters*, 1909–1914, ed. Omar

Pound and A. Walton Litz (London, 1985), pp.82, 84; and see Noel Stock, *The Life of Ezra Pound* (Harmondsworth, 1985), p.25.
15 See Daniel Pearlman, *The Barb of Time* (New York, 1969), pp.299–303; *Poetry*, 10, nos.3–5 (June–July–August 1917); and *Quia Pauper Amavi* (London, 1919).
16 *The Cantos* contain many more passages of stray allusions to painters and works of art than I have space to examine here. Donald Davie's discussion of Canto XVII in relation to Venetian sculpture and architecture is in *Ezra Pound: Poet as Sculptor* (London, 1965), pp.127–32; D. G. Bridson, 'Italian Painting in The Cantos', in *Agenda*, 17, no.3–4 – 18, no.1 (Autumn–Winter–Spring, 1979–80), pp.210–17 has much useful information and a discussion of an important passage in Canto XX which I do not touch on. Hugh Kenner, *The Pound Era* (London, 1972) is the principal source for information about Pound's emblematic art works.
17 *The Cantos of Ezra Pound*, 3rd edn (London, 1975), p.11.
18 *Their Letters*, p.33.
19 'Three Cantos', I, in *Poetry*, 10, no.3 (June 1917), p.116.

20 *Ibid.*, p.117.
21 *Ibid.*, p.118.
22 *Ibid.*, p.120.
23 *Ibid.*, pp.120–1. The allusion to '(Simonetta?)' may indicate the influence of Walter Pater's essay on Botticelli in *The Renaissance*, ed. Donald L. Hall (Berkeley and Los Angeles, Calif., 1980), p.47, and p.339n., where he notes of the Venus in 'La Nascita di Venere' ('The Birth of Venus'):

> The same figure – tradition connects it with Simonetta, the mistress of Giuliano de' Medici – appears again as Judith, returning home across the hill country, when the great deed is over, and the moment of revulsion come, when the olive branch in her hand is becoming a burthen; as *Justice*, sitting on a throne, but with a fixed look of self-hatred which makes the sword in her hand seem that of a suicide, and again as *Veritas*, in the allegorical picture of *Calumnia*, where one may note in passing the suggestiveness of an accident which identifies the image of Truth with the person of Venus.

24 *Literary Essays*, p.154.
25 For the source of this line in the works of Poggio, see Carroll F. Terrell, *A Companion to the Cantos of Ezra Pound* (Berkeley and Los Angeles, Calif., 1980), p.9.
26 'Three Cantos', I, p.121.
27 *Quia Pauper Amavi*, p.23; and see *L'opera completa del Mantegna*, ed. Bellonci and Garavaglia (Milan, 1967), pp.100–8.
28 *Cantos*, p.12.
29 Pearlman, p.53.
30 D. S. Chambers, *Patrons and Artists in the Italian Renaissance* (London, 1970), p.125.
31 *Ibid.*, pp.124 and 125.
32 Zinnes, p.297.
33 Giorgio Vasari, *The Lives of the Artists*, trans. George Bull (Harmondsworth, 1965), pp.241, 244.
34 Chambers, p.117.
35 Michael Baxandall, *Painting and Experience in Fifteenth Century Italy* (Oxford, 1972), p.12.
36 *ABC of Reading* (London, 1961), p.30 and, for his translation of the letter, see *Cantos*, pp.125–6; Pisanello has numerous representations of horses: see, for example, nos. 55–64 in *L'opera completa del Pisanello*, ed. Dell' Acqua and Chiarelli (Milan, 1972), pp.92–4; Pound refers to

him as a medallist in *Cantos*, pp.437, 447, 448, and see *L'opera*, pp.96–101; he alludes to a portrait of Lionello d'Este in *Cantos*, p.462, which is no.88 in *L'opera*, p.97.
37 Baxandall, p.14.
38 See Chambers, pp.163–4.
39 Peter d'Epiro, *A Touch of Rhetoric: Ezra Pound's Malatesta Cantos* (Epping, 1983), p.xviii.
40 *Cantos*, p.24.
41 *Ibid.*, p.28.
42 *Ibid.*, p.29; in Franco Borsi, *Leon Battista Alberti* (London, 1977), the translation suggests rather that the painter would first finish the chapels than do other work: 'After he has painted these chapels, I shall want him to paint other things, such as will give both him and me great pleasure', p.128.
43 *Cantos*, p.29.
44 *Ibid.*, p.97; in Canto VIII the phrase is quoted as 'piacere o no'.
45 Borsi, p.128.
46 *Guide to Kulchur* (New York, 1968), p.159.
47 *Selected Letters of Ezra Pound, 1907–1941* (London, 1982), p.212; there seems no evidence to suggest that Mino da Fiesole worked for Sigismondo Malatesta. The explanation for Pound's citing him may be a portrait bust of Lucrezia Tornabuoni in Pisa once considered an authentic piece by Mino and a portrait of Isotta. See Gianni Carlo Sciolla, *La Scultura di Mino da Fiesole* (Turin, 1970), pp.117–18; and the line 'Divae Ixottae (and as to her effigy that was in Pisa?)', *Cantos*, p.459.
48 Pound's critics have advanced a number of explanations for the definition of 'usury' in his work. Canto XLV has a footnote to assist us: 'N.B. Usury: A charge for the use of purchasing power, levied without regard to production; often without regard to the possibilities of production. (Hence the failure of the Medici bank.)' (*Cantos*, p.230.) Hugh Kenner relates it to Douglasite economics (see note 3, p.23 of this catalogue) in *The Pound Era*, p.407. Donald Davie relates it to sculptural values in *Poet as Sculptor*, p.159. A recent volume examining these matters is Peter Nicholls, *Ezra Pound: Politics, Economics and Writing* (London, 1984).
49 *Cantos*, p.229.
50 Zinnes, p.173. For further details on the Palazzo Pubblico in Siena, see Bridson, pp.210–11; and the *Guide to Kulchur*, p.113.

51 *Cantos*, p.230.
52 *Ibid.*, p.119.
53 *Chambers*, p.82; the painting has since been destroyed, but two reproductions of copies may be found in Harold E. Wethey, *The Paintings of Titian*, 3 vols. (London, 1969–75), vol.3, figs.51–2; Wethey rejects the idea of rivalry between Titian and Bellini in vol.1, pp.10–11.
54 *Cantos*, p.119.
55 *Ibid.*, p.120.
56 Wethey, vol.3, p.228.
57 *Cantos*, p.127.
58 Chambers, pp.123–4.
59 *L'opera completa del Carpaccio*, ed. M. Cancogni and G. Perocco (Milan, 1967), p.84.
60 See Terrell, p.109, who notes that 'The real letter is firm about Mozart's desire to leave but is quite politely worded.'
61 *ABC of Reading*, p.134; this work by Perugino may be a 'Cristo nel Sarcofago' in the Galleria Nazionale dell' Umbria, Perugia, and no.49A in *L'opera completa del Perugino*, ed. Castellaneta and Camesasca (Milan, 1969), p.95.
62 *Selected Prose 1909–1965*, ed. William Cookson (London, 1973), p.200.
63 D'Epiro, p.105.
64 *Selected Prose*, p.200.
65 *Gaudier*, p.48.
66 Dante, *Purgatorio*, XXVI, l.117.
67 *The Spirit of Romance* (New York, 1968), p.22; at this time Pound may have also seen the 'Madonna in a Rose Garden' by Stefano da Verona (1374–1438), now in the Museo del Castelvecchio, Verona, and alluded to in *Cantos*, pp.16 and 448.
68 Stock, p.107.
69 Zinnes, p.173. Pound may be conflating two sculptors: 'Adimarus de S. Giorgio', architect of the crypt, and Guillelmus, who sculpted the left side of the main entrance. See H. Decker, *Romanesque Art in Italy* (London, 1958), pp.78–9.
70 *Cantos*, p.230.
71 Zinnes, p.173.
72 John Ruskin, *Works*, ed. Cook and Wedderburn, Library Edition, 39 vols. (London, 1903–12), vol.9, p.379; the analogy between twisted columns and tree-trunks is discussed at pp.357–8; he discusses the entrance on p.214.
73 Ruskin, vol.10, p.192.
74 Ruskin, vol.11, p.102.
75 *Cantos*, p.176.
76 Ruskin, vol.11, p.103.

77 *Ibid.*, p.105.
78 *Literary Essays*, p.153.
79 Zinnes, p.139.
80 *Cantos*, p.122.
81 *Ibid.*, p.228.
82 *Ibid.*, p.213; and see Cancogni and Perocco, pp.94–5.
83 Peter Faulkner, 'Pound and the Pre-Raphaelites', in *Paideuma*, 13, no.2 (Fall 1984), p.237.
84 Zinnes, p.76.
85 *Ibid.*, p.77. Pound remarks on a San Zeno in concrete in *Their Letters*, p.199.
86 Pound visited Santa Maria dei Miracoli in 1913, though he may have seen it earlier; see *Their Letters*, pp.226, 227, and *Cantos*, pp.229, 430, 460, 529.
87 Ruskin, vol.16, p.324.
88 *Ibid.*, p.320.
89 Zinnes, pp.85–6. See also p.76 of this catalogue.
90 Ruskin, vol.10, p.202.
91 *Cantos*, pp.229–30.
92 *Guide to Kulchur*, p.113; and see *Cantos*, p.462 where the work referred to is the 'Pala di Cortona', no.28 in *L'opera completa dell' Angelico*, ed. Morante and Baldini (Milan, 1970), pp.92–3.
93 *Cantos*, p.230.
94 Anthony Blunt, *Artistic Theory in Italy 1450–1600* (Oxford, 1940), p.49.
95 *Ibid.*, p.10.
96 Zinnes, p.173.
97 Chambers, p.182.
98 *Ibid.*, p.162.
99 *Ibid.*, p.163.
100 *Cantos*, p.792.
101 Baxandall, p.18.
102 D. R. Edward Wright, 'Alberti's *De Pictura*', in *Journal of the Warburg and Courtauld Institutes*, 47 (1984), p.67.
103 Bridson, p.216.
104 Alberti, *De Pictura*, cited in Roberto Salvini, *All the Paintings of Botticelli*, 4 vols. (London, 1965), vol.4, p.161.
105 *Cantos*, p.481.
106 Pater, p.47.
107 Vasari, cited in Roberto Salvini, vol.4, p.161.
108 *Cantos*, p.229.
109 *Cantos*, p.41.
110 Borsi, p.138.
111 Terrell, p.49.
112 Borsi, p.376.
113 *Literary Essays*, p.154.
114 *Spirit of Romance*, p.22; and see *Cantos*, p.448. Pound's liking for early

architecture is also evident in his
evocation of Torcello in *Cantos*, pp.777, 780.

[115] Zinnes, pp.167–8.

[116] Terrell, p.49.

[117] Adrian Stokes, 'The Sculptor Agostino di
Duccio', in *The Criterion*, 9, no.34 (October
1929), p.44; there is not space to look at
Pound's interests in Byzantine
architecture and decoration here. For the
importance of the Tomb of Galla Placidia,
Ravenna, see Charles Tomlinson, *Some
Americans* (Berkeley and Los Angeles,
Calif., 1981), pp.103–7; Pound
comments on the significance to him of
mosaics in Santa Maria in Trastevere,
Rome, in *Selected Prose*, p.290.

[118] For relations between Stokes and Pound,
see Donald Davie's pioneering essay,
'Adrian Stokes and Pound's "Cantos"', in
The Twentieth Century, 160, no.957
(November 1956), pp.418–36; Richard
Wollheim, 'Introduction' to Adrian Stokes,
The Image in Form (Harmondsworth,
1972), p.12; and Richard Read, 'Adrian
Stokes: a biography with bibliography' in
Adrian Stokes, Catalogue to the Serpentine
exhibition of his paintings (London,
1982), p.52.

[119] *Cantos*, p.36.

[120] Terrell, p.45.

[121] Zinnes, p.168.

[122] Davie, *Poet as Sculptor*, p.218.

[123] Zinnes, p.137.

[124] *Selected Letters*, p.254.

[125] Pater, p.106.

[126] Zinnes, p.137.

[127] Adrian Stokes, *The Critical Writings*, 3 vols.
(London, 1978), vol.1, p.236.

[128] David Anderson, 'Breaking the Silence', in
Paideuma, 10, no.2 (1981), p.341.

[129] See Pound's remark on Benito Mussolini
in *Jefferson and/or Mussolini* (London,
1935), p.34: 'Treat him as *artifex* and all
the details fall into place. Take him as
anything save the artist and you will get
muddled with contradictions.'

[130] Zinnes, p.305, and, for following citation,
ibid., p.168.

[131] Cited in Baxandall, p.56.

[132] *Guide to Kulchur*, prefatory note, no page
number; and see no.70 in *L'opera completa
di Giovanni Bellini*, ed. Ghiotto and Pignatti
(Milan, 1969), p.94.

[133] Pater, p.39.

[134] Kenneth Clark, *Piero della Francesca*
(London, 1969), p.31.

[135] Four citations from Adrian Stokes,

[136] *Literary Essays*, p.4.

[137] K. M. Clark, review of *The Quattro Cento* by
Adrian Stokes, in *The Criterion* (October,
1932), p.148.

[138] *Literary Essays*, p.152.

[139] *Ibid.*, p.153.

[140] *Ibid.*

[141] Kenneth Clark, *The Nude*
(Harmondsworth, 1960), p.328.

[142] *Literary Essays*, p.153.

[143] *Ibid.*

[144] *Ibid.*

[145] *Cantos*, p.511.

[146] Bridson, p.212, and see *Their Letters*,
pp.120–1.

[147] *Shorter Poems*, p.73.

[148] Martin Davies, *The Early Italian Schools*,
2nd edn (London, 1961), p.116.

[149] For an example of a writer arguing at
approximately this time for a controlled
tolerance of usury, see Francis Bacon, 'On
Usury', in *Essays*, intro. M. J. Hawkins
(London, 1972), pp.123–6.

[150] *Selected Prose*, p.330.

[151] 'René Crevel', *The Criterion* (January
1939), p.235.

[152] *Selected Prose*, p.293; Pound is aware that
'"The character of the man is revealed in
every brush-stroke["?] (and this does not
apply only to ideograms).' Yet, as far as I
am aware, he nowhere confronts the
question of how, and how directly, an
economic system determines the character
of a work of art, or whether an individual
artist can act independently of the
determining conditions.

[153] *Ibid.*, pp.24, 25.

[154] *Literary Essays*, p.420.

[155] Zinnes, p.305; Pound singles out
Carpaccio's 'San Giorgio in lotta col drago'
from the frescoes in the Scuola di San
Giorgio degli Schiavoni, in *Cantos*, p.461,
and no.33G in *L'opera*, pp.99–100.

[156] *Guide to Kulchur*, pp.110–11; for Pound's
most intemperate remark on Rembrandt,
see 'Ezra Pound on Wyndham Lewis's *The
Hitler Cult*', in *Blast 3*, ed. Seamus Cooney
(Santa Barbara, 1984), p.185.

[157] Bridson, p.216.

[158] *Ibid.*, p.214.

[159] *Cantos*, p.229.

[160] *Guide to Kulchur*, p.109.

[161] *Cantos*, pp.229–30.

[162] *Guide to Kulchur*, p.159.

[163] *Selected Letters*, p.239.

[164] Mary de Rachewiltz, 'Fragments of an Atmosphere', in *Agenda*, 17, nos. 3–4–18, no. 1 (Autumn–Winter–Spring 1979–80), p.166 (twice).

[165] *Cantos*, p.51.

[166] Stock, p.519.

[167] *Cantos*, p.425.

[168] *Ibid.*, p.459.

[169] *Ibid.*, p.497, and see *Selected Prose*, pp.282–3.

[170] *Cantos*, p.478, and see *America, Roosevelt and the Causes of the Present War*, trans. J. Drummond (London, 1951), pp.6–7.

[171] *Jefferson and/or Mussolini*, p.33.

[172] Denis Mack Smith, *Mussolini* (London, 1983), p.352.

[173] *Cantos*, p.427.

[174] By concentrating here on Pound's relations with Olga Rudge I do not mean to imply that other women important in his life are not also involved in these cantos. The poet H.D., for example, is understood to be honoured in the 'Lynx-hymn' of Canto LXXIX; see *Cantos*, pp.487–92 and H.D., *An End to Torment* (New York, 1979), p.17.

[175] Stokes, vol. 1, p.294 (three times).

[176] *Cantos*, p.459.

[177] *Cantos*, p.521.

[178] See Davie, *Poet as Sculptor*, p.156.

[179] *Cantos*, p.430; in some editions 'Pietro Romano' is correctly printed as 'Pietro Lombardo'.

[180] *Cantos*, p.529.

[181] See Mary de Rachewiltz, *Discretions* (London, 1971), pp.150–1 and 257–8.

[182] *Cantos*, p.444.

[183] *Ibid.*, p.446.

[184] *Shorter Poems*, p.200.

[185] *Ibid.*, p.198.

[186] *Cantos*, p.510.

[187] *Ibid.*, p.511.

[188] *Ibid.*, p.519.

[189] *Shorter Poems*, p.200.

[190] *Cantos*, p.539.

[191] See Mack Smith, p.356.

[192] Stock, p.347.

[193] W. B. Yeats, *A Vision* (London, 1937), p.5.

[194] See Pearlman, p.294.

[195] *Cantos*, p.475.

[196] See *L'opera completa di Cosmè Tura . . .*, ed. R. Molajoli (Milan, 1974), pp.100–2.

[197] *Cantos*, p.114; Terrell, p.99, notes that 'Julia the Countess' was probably a 'member of the Tassoni family of Ferrara, which owned the Schifanoia at one time' and he points out that the place was once used as a tobacco factory, adding 'the Italian verb, *conciare*, means to tan hides, or to cure tobacco, hence the confusion of *tannery* in the text'.

[198] *Cantos*, pp.95, 96.

[199] Pearlman, p.296.

[200] *Cantos*, p.443.

[201] *Ibid.*, p.473.

[202] *Ibid.*, p.475.

[203] *Ibid.*, p.477.

[204] *Ibid.*, p.484.

[205] *Ibid.*, p.485.

[206] Stock, p.530.

[207] Zinnes, p.101.

[208] 'Pound's Interrogation at Genoa', in *Helix* (Australia), 13 and 14 (1983), p.131.

[209] Davie, *Poet as Sculptor*, p.181.